Welcome to English
BOOK 1

WELCOME TO ENGLISH

BOOK 1

WILLARD D. SHEELER

OXFORD UNIVERSITY PRESS
Ely House, London W1X 4AH
200 Madison Avenue, New York, N.Y. 10016

ENGLISH LANGUAGE SERVICES, INC.
14350 N.W. Science Park Drive, Portland, Oregon 97229

Copyright © English Language Services, Inc. 1976

Library of Congress Catalog Card Number 75-10596

All rights reserved. No part of this book may be reproduced or transmitted in any form or by any means, electronic or mechanical, including photocopying, recording or by any information storage and retrieval system, without permission in advance in writing from the publisher, English Language Services Inc. World distribution rights are held by Oxford University Press.

ELS ISBN 0 89285 005 1
OUP ISBN 0 19 433600 x

Printed in the United States of America

PREFACE

Welcome to English is an adult course for learners of English as a foreign or second language. Each of the six basic texts consists of twenty-four lessons. These 144 lessons take the learner from the very beginning to a knowledge and control of a great many of the most essential structures of the language.

This series of books is a successor to *Intensive Course in English* which has been and continues to be used in a wide variety of situations throughout the world. *Welcome to English* retains the same basic ordering of structural points (with some important additions) and makes use of most of the same high frequency vocabulary as used in *Intensive Course in English*. The present books, however, are new in content, organization and approach.

Welcome to English endeavors to develop four language skills. Speaking and understanding are stressed in the basic textbooks; reading and writing skills are emphasized in both the collateral *Reading and Writing Workbooks** and in the *Reading and Exercise Series*. For learners of the English alphabet, there is one book giving practice in the recognition and writing of the English letters.*

The lessons of the basic texts are constructed with the principles of naturalness, variety and development in mind. The development of basic vocabulary and structure proceeds at an orderly pace, but the dialogs and readings are not slaves to this progression. On the contrary, they aim at natural English and include some non-basic vocabulary and sometimes anticipate structures to be taught later.

The inclusion of some variety in the text lessons was a writing aim. Each lesson has dialogs (and/or readings) and exercises, but they are not arranged in the same order each time and there is considerable variance among them. Some dialogs the student should listen to and repeat; others he need only listen to for comprehension and learn the new words. (Sometimes these are ones in which a child does much of the speaking and which are not so useful to imitate.)

With reference to the dialogs, the introductory background notes in the early lessons must be translated for the student as they include both vocabulary and structures not included in the course of study at that point. The dialogs themselves, of course, must also be explained or translated and analyzed for the student to insure that he understands fully what he is learning. Meaning should never be subordinated to other considerations.

A Listening Practice ends every unit of the textbooks. The dialogs for listening contain nothing new to the student, but give him a situation that he should understand easily. In the first books, the listening practices are printed in the text; in later volumes, the visual material (except for pictures) is gradually withdrawn. The readings in the text are intended primarily to be used for comprehension practice and as the basis for answering comprehension questions.

The exercises include repetition, simple and progressive substitution, completion, combination, expansion, response and comprehension. One format that should be noted is the Speaker A/Speaker B type. In these, one speaker asks a question and the second speaker replies according to the 'statement of fact' given in the book. On tape the student is told which speaker's part to take, but in class he can do either part, or two students can participate in the drill.

Each drill bears a grammatical title but there are very few grammar explanations in the texts. It is left to the teacher to explain grammar in line with his or her pedagogical preferences and at a time of his or her own choosing.

The accompanying *Teacher's Manuals** provide grammar summaries and notes for teacher reference. The manuals also contain expansions of many of the short drills which appear in the course, have summary vocabularies, list the high-frequency words in each lesson and provide a number of consolidation drills. A substantial number of review exercises and a 50-item checkup follow each 12 lessons of Books 1-4. These are printed in separate booklets and are accompanied by pre-recorded tapes. The checkups alone are reprinted in the appropriate teacher's manuals.

Stress and intonation is selectively marked in all six books with arrows down (↘) and up (↗) placed over the word that bears the sentence stress and where there is a change in pitch. Systematic coverage of the vowels and consonants begins in Book 2.

In the dialogs and readings a small group of people (different in Books 1 and 2) provides continuity through their enactment of a subdued on-going story line. This development and continuity gives a concrete set of situations and story characters to discuss in class. The pictures also provide a source of learning and conversational material over and above the actual content of the dialogs and readings.

Each of the six texts is accompanied by pre-recorded tapes prepared under the direction of Bobby J. Simpson in the ELS Recording Studios.

The pronunciation sections in Books 2-4 were written by Rayner W. Markley, who also provided valuable criticism and gave assistance with the various textbooks and auxiliary materials.

---

*Forthcoming titles

CONTENTS

UNIT 1   1-31

Grammar and Pronunciation

    BE: Affirmative Statement, Yes/No Question,
         Question-word (Wh-) Questions (who/what),
         Affirmative Short Answer
    I/you/we/they + Main Verb
    This/these/that/those
    Intonation: Yes/No and Wh- Questions
    Pronunciation: Noun Plurals and Noun Compounds
    Vocabulary: Professions

Lesson 1:	An Office Visitor	2
Lesson 2:	Old Friends	6
Lesson 3:	Old Friends Talk	14
Lesson 4:	The Dinner Guest	22

UNIT 2   32-63

Grammar and Pronunciation

    BE: Negative Statement, Negative Question,
         Negative Short Answers
    Irregular Noun Plurals
    Identification: Who/What
    Conjunction with *and*
    Names in English

Lesson 5:	Visitors	33
Lesson 6:	Getting Acquainted; Mrs. Watson and Her Family	39
Lesson 7:	Visiting	46
Lesson 8:	Introducing Jim	53

UNIT 3
Grammar and Pronunciation 64-92

BE: Past Tense, Affirmative Statement,
  Negative Statement, Yes/No and Wh-
  Questions (when), Short Answers
  (Affirmative and Negative)
Cardinal Numbers 1-100/Ordinal Numbers
Years/Months/Dates/Ages
Street Addresses
Conjunction with *and... too, but*
Questions with *Do* and *Does*

Lesson 9:	Talking About the Carlsons	65
Lesson 10:	Six Conversations	72
Lesson 11:	Rodney Hill Watson	79
Lesson 12:	Dinner Party at the Watsons'	86

UNIT 4
Grammar and Pronunciation 93-138

Present and Past Continuous: Affirmative Statement,
  Negative Statement, Yes/No and Wh- Questions,
  Short Answers
Time of Day/Days of the Week
Cities/Countries/Nationalities

Lesson 13:	Jim Carter; Mrs. Watson Comes Home	94
Lesson 14:	Telephone Conversation	105
Lesson 15:	What Day Is It?	114
Lesson 16:	A Dinner Party	126

UNIT 5
Grammar and Pronunciation 139-179

Tag Questions with *BE:* Present and Past,
  Affirmative and Negative
There is/there are...
Possessive Determiners: my/your/his/her...
Count and Mass Nouns: Definite/Indefinite

Lesson 17:	The Efficient Secretary; At the Meeting	140
Lesson 18:	Morning in the Watson Household	149
Lesson 19:	A Letter to Jim	159
Lesson 20:	Getting Lunch: Lunch is Served; Alice and Anita	169

UNIT 6   180-220

Grammar and Pronunciation

    The 'going to' Future: Affirmative and Negative
        Statements, Yes/No, Wh-, and Tag Questions
    Countries/Nationalities
    First Names: Diminutive Forms
    Greetings/Departures/Responses

Lesson 21:	Surprising News; Getting Ready for the Trip	180
Lesson 22:	Driving to the Airport; At the Airport	190
Lesson 23:	A Letter to Alice; Meeting on the Street	199
Lesson 24:	At the Airport	211

Appendix	222
Index	226
Grammar Points	230
Vocabulary	237

Welcome to English
BOOK 1

UNIT 1

THE PEOPLE IN UNIT 1

Some characters appear many times in this book. They appear in all of the dialogs, in some of the readings and in a few of the exercises. The members of the Watson family are the most important characters. Below are pictures of them. There are also pictures of other characters in Unit 1.

THE WATSON FAMILY

ROBERT WATSON
(husband)
Age 35
Biologist

ELLIE WATSON
(daughter)
Age 10
Student in
elementary school

BARBARA WATSON
(wife)
Age 29
Nurse

TOM WATSON
(son)
Age 4
Student in
nursery school

WILLIAM SMITH
(friend of
the Watsons)
Age 36
Lawyer

MISS BETTY GREEN
(works in Mr. Smith's
law office)
Age 47
Secretary

MISS ANN LONG
(works in Mr. Smith's
law office)
Age 23
Typist

LESSON 1

DIALOG: AN OFFICE VISITOR

Mr. Smith and Mr. Watson are old friends. Not long ago Mr. Smith moved to Madison. Mr. Watson lives in Madison, too. Mr. Watson made an appointment to see Mr. Smith in his office. They are going to have lunch.

SECRETARY	Good morning.
MR. WATSON	Good morning.
SECRETARY	May I help you?
MR. WATSON	Yes, please. Is Mr. Smith in?
SECRETARY	Yes, he is. Are you Mr. Watson?
MR. WATSON	Yes, I am.

PRACTICE DRILLS AND EXERCISES

First listen to the sentences. Then repeat them.

1 Greetings

SPEAKER A

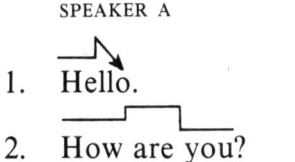

1. Hello.
2. How are you?

3. Fine, thanks.

SPEAKER B

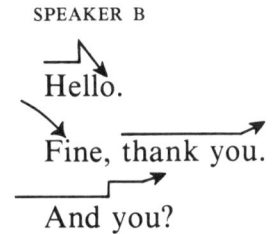

Hello.
Fine, thank you.
And you?

2 Greetings

TEACHER

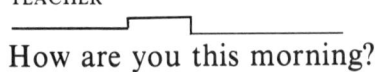

How are you this morning?

STUDENT

Fine, thank you.
Just fine, thank you.
I'm fine, thank you.
Very well, thank you.

3 Greetings

TEACHER

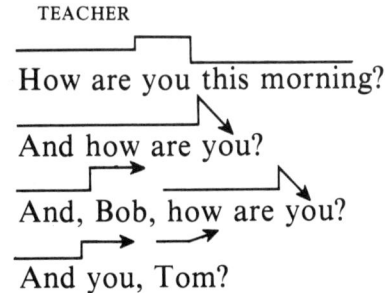

How are you this morning?
And how are you?
And, Bob, how are you?
And you, Tom?

STUDENT

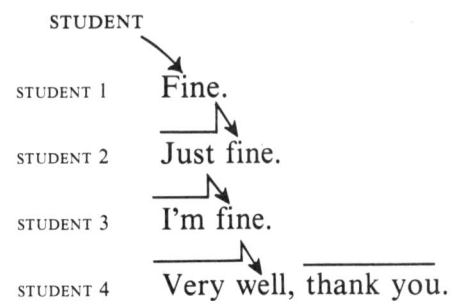

STUDENT 1   Fine.
STUDENT 2   Just fine.
STUDENT 3   I'm fine.
STUDENT 4   Very well, thank you.

4 Intonation: Yes/No questions

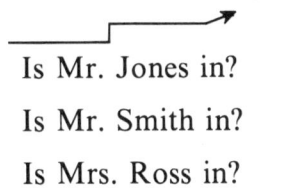

Is Mr. Jones in?
Is Mr. Smith in?
Is Mrs. Ross in?

Are you Mr. Watson?
Are you Miss Green?
Are you Mrs. Smith?

BASIC SENTENCES

Listen to these sentences. Then repeat them.

1. My name is Robert Watson.
2. I am a scientist.

3. This is Miss Green
4. She's a secretary.

5. This is Mr. Smith.
6. He is a lawyer.
7. He's my friend.

8. That is Miss Long.
9. She is a typist.

NEW VOCABULARY IN LESSON 1*

NOUNS	VERBS	ADJECTIVE	ADVERBS
friend secretary lawyer student morning teacher name typist office visitor scientist	BE: am are is help	good	fine in just well

GRAMMAR WORDS	COMPOUND	TITLES & NAMES

Article: a
Demonstrative Pronouns:
    that   this
Response Word: yes
Question Word: how
Conjunction: and
Subject Pronouns:
    he   she
    I   you
Object Pronoun: you
Contractions:
    he's   I'm
Possessive Determiner:
    my
Intensifier: very
	office visitor
	
	EXPRESSIONS
	
	Good morning.
	Hello.
	How are you?
	Just fine.
	May I help you?
	Thank you.
	Thanks.
	Yes, please.
	Very well.
		Titles:
		    Mr. Miss Mrs.
		Family Names:
		    Green Ross
		    Jones Smith
		    Long Watson
		Masculine Names:
		    Bob Tom
		    Robert

*All new vocabulary words are categorized according to how they are used in the lesson.

LESSON 2

DIALOG: OLD FRIENDS

Mr. William (Bill) Smith comes out of his office and greets his old friend, Robert (Bob) Watson.

MR. SMITH	Hello, Bob. How are you?
MR. WATSON	Fine, Bill. It's good to see you again.
MR. SMITH	Come in. Come in.
MR. WATSON	Say, this is a nice office!
MR. SMITH	Thanks. Sit down. How's your family?

PRACTICE DRILLS AND EXERCISES (1)

Listen to these sentences. Then repeat them.

1 *BE:* **Contraction** *I'm*

I'm Bill Smith. I'm a lawyer.

I'm Barbara Watson. I'm a nurse.

I'm Eric Carlson. I'm a scientist.

I'm Kathy Johnson. I'm a student.

2 *BE:* **Contractions** *You're/He's/She's*

(a)	(b)	(c)
You're *a lawyer.*	He's *a teacher.*	She's *a doctor.*
You're *a teacher.*	He's *a professor.*	She's *a typist.*
You're *a doctor.*	He's *a dentist.*	She's *a secretary.*
You're *a dentist.*	He's *a doctor.*	She's *a scientist.*

3 Pronoun Substitution: *He/She*

First study these names.

MASCULINE NAMES	FEMININE NAMES
Mr. Watson	Mrs. Watson
Mr. Smith	Miss Long
	Ms. Brown
Jim Nelson	Betty Fuller
John Carter	Jane Carlson
Bob	Barbara
Tom	Ellie

Now do the exercise. Use *he's* or *she's*.

1. This is Mr. Watson. *He's* a scientist.
2. This is Betty. *She's* a secretary.
3. This is Jim Nelson. . . . . . a professor.
4. This is Miss Long. . . . . . a typist.
5. This is Tom. . . . . . a student.
6. This is Barbara Watson. . . . . . a nurse.
7. This is John. . . . . . a student.
8. This is John Carter. . . . . . a lawyer.
9. This is Bob. . . . . . a scientist.
10. This is Ms. Brown. . . . . . a teacher.

4 Imperative: Useful Expressions

Repeat these expressions.

(a) Listen.
Listen and repeat.
Repeat after me.

Repeat the word.
Repeat the sentence.

(b) Open your book.
Close your book.
Please close your book.

Start your tape recorder.
Stop your tape recorder.

QUESTIONS AND ANSWERS

Listen to these questions and answers. Then repeat them.

1. Who's this?
   a. That's Mr. Watson.
   b. He's a scientist.

2. Who's that?
   a. That's Betty Green.
   b. She's a secretary.

3. Who are you?
   a. I'm Jane Brown.
   b. I'm a lawyer.

4. Who's that boy over there?
   a. That's Bob Long.
   b. He's a new student.

5. Who's that man?
   a. That's Mr. Ross.
   b. He's a professor.

6. Who's that woman?
   a. That's Mrs. Smith.
   b. She's a typist.

PRACTICE DRILLS AND EXERCISES (2)

1 Identifying People

Take the part of Speaker B.

MR. LONG IS A SCIENTIST.

A Who's this?

B *That's Mr. Long. He's a scientist.*

MISS SMITH IS A NURSE.

A Who's that?

B *That's Miss Smith. She's a nurse.*

TOM BROWN IS A STUDENT.

A Who's that man?

B *That's Tom Brown. He's a student.*

4. MISS NELSON IS A SECRETARY.

A Who's that woman?

B ....

5. MR. SMITH IS A LAWYER.

A Who's that?

B ....

6. MR. NELSON IS A SCIENTIST.

A Who's that man over there?

B ....

7. MISS RAMOS IS A DOCTOR.

A Who's that woman?

B ....

UNIT 1 LESSON 2 | 11

2 Contractions with BE: I'm/He's/She's

Take the part of the student.

	TEACHER	STUDENT
1.	How's Miss Long?	*She's fine, thank you.*
2.	How are you?	*I'm fine, thank you.*
3.	How's Bob?	....
4.	How's Mr. Watson?	....
5.	How's Ellie?	....
6.	How's Betty?	....
7.	How's Jim Nelson?	....
8.	How's Miss Green?	....
9.	How's Tom?	....
10.	How are you?	....

NEW VOCABULARY IN LESSON 2

NOUNS		VERBS		ADJECTIVES	ADVERBS
book	nurse	close	sit	new	again
boy	professor	come	sit down	nice	down
dentist	sentence	come in	start	old	over
doctor	tape	listen	stop		there
family	woman	open			
girl	word	repeat			
man		see			

GRAMMAR WORDS	COMPOUND	TITLE & NAMES
Question Word: who	tape recorder	Title: Ms.
Possessive Determiner: your		Family Names:
Demonstrative Determiner: that	EXPRESSIONS	Brown Johnson Carlson Nelson Carter Ramos Fuller
Contractions: it's how's who's she's that's you're	It's good to see you. Say! over there Repeat after me.	Masculine Names: Bill Jim Eric John
Infinitive Particle: to Subject Pronoun: it		Feminine Names: Barbara Jane Betty Kathy Ellie

LESSON 3

BASIC SENTENCES

Listen to these sentences. Then repeat them.

1. I'm a lawyer.
2. You're a lawyer, too.
3. We're lawyers.
4. We practice law.

5. Tom's an engineer.
6. Bill's an engineer, too.
7. They're engineers.
8. They're good engineers.

9. Mr. Todd's an artist.
10. Miss Platte's an artist, too.
11. He's an artist and she's an artist, too.
12. They're artists.

PRONUNCIATION PRACTICE

1 Pronunciation of Contractions with *BE*: /s/ and /z/

Listen. Then repeat.

/s/	/z/
Mr. Watson's a scientist.	Tom's an engineer.
Eric's my friend.	Betty's a scientist.
Robert's a fine boy.	He's over here.
The student's here now.	She's Miss Green.

2   Pronunciation of Noun Plurals: /s/, /z/, and /iz/

Listen. Then repeat.

/s/		/z/		/iz/	
book	books	boy	boys	nurse	nurses
tape	tapes	name	names	office	offices
student	students	friend	friends	class	classes
artist	artists	doctor	doctors		

PRACTICE DRILLS AND EXERCISES

1   BE: Full Forms and Contractions

First listen to the sentences. Then repeat them.

FULL FORMS	CONTRACTIONS
I am here.	I'm here.
They are lawyers.	They're lawyers.
He is a doctor.	He's a doctor.
We are here.	We're here.
You are young.	You're young.
She is a nurse.	She's a nurse.
It is new.	It's new.
That is my sister.	That's my sister.
You are brothers.	You're brothers.

Complete the sentences. Use contractions.

1. I am here.
   I'm here.

2. You are my friend.
   . . . . . . my best friend.

3. We are Tom Brown and Jack Carter.
   . . . . . . students.

4. They are Barbara and Jane.
   . . . . . . good friends.

5. She is a doctor.
   . . . . . . my doctor.

6. He is a professor.
   . . . . . . a law professor.

7. It is a book.
   . . . . . . a very good book.

8. I am a student.
   . . . . . . a new student.

2 **BE: Contractions** *We're/ You're/ They're*

First, listen to the models. Then repeat the third sentence.

1. I'm a lawyer.
   You're a lawyer, too.
   We're lawyers.

2. You're a student.
   I'm a student, too.
   We're students.

3. He's an artist.
   She's an artist, too.
   They're artists.

4. Betty's my friend.
   Jane's my friend, too.
   They're my friends.

5. You're an engineer.
   Tom's an engineer, too.
   You're engineers.

6. I'm a visitor here.
   You're a visitor here, too.
   We're visitors here.

7. He's my brother.
   And *he's* my brother, too.
   They're my brothers.

8. She's my sister.
   And *she's* my sister, too.
   They're my sisters.

9. He's my brother.
   And she's my sister.
   They're my brother and sister.

10. They're my brothers.
    They're my sisters.
    They're my brothers and sisters.

11. They're professors.
    We're professors, too.
    We're professors.

12. He's a young person.
    She's a young person, too.
    They're young people.

3 Use of *an* Before Vowels

Repeat these phrases.

an artist	a nurse
an engineer	a secretary
an old friend	a new teacher

Fill the blanks with *a* or *an* and repeat the sentence.

1. He's ...... doctor.
2. She's ...... nurse.
3. It's ...... old book.
4. He's ...... artist.
5. They're ...... nice family.
6. It's ...... office.
7. He's ...... visitor.
8. She's ...... English teacher.

4 *BE:* Contractions *We're/They're/You're*

Use *we're/they're/you're* as subjects.

1. Jane's an artist.
   Jim's an artist, too.
   They're artists.
   ....

2. Mr. Watson's a scientist.
   Mr. Carlson's a scientist, too.
   ....

3. I'm a student.
   You're a student, too.

   . . . .

4. Tom's her brother.
   Bill's her brother, too.

   . . . .

5. You're my friend.
   Betty's my friend, too.

   . . . .

6. Jane's my sister.
   Betty's my sister, too.

   . . . .

7. I'm here.
   He's here, too.

   . . . .

8. Miss Green's a typist.
   I'm a typist, too.

   . . . .

9. You're a professor.
   He's a professor, too.

   . . . .

10. He's my brother.
    She's my sister.

    . . . .

INTONATION: YES/ NO QUESTIONS

Listen. Then repeat after Speaker A.

SPEAKER A	SPEAKER B
Is that your brother?	Yes, it is.
Is that your sister?	Yes, it is.
Is he a doctor?	Yes, he is.
Are you a lawyer?	Yes, I am.
Is she a teacher?	Yes, she is.

CONVERSATION PRACTICE

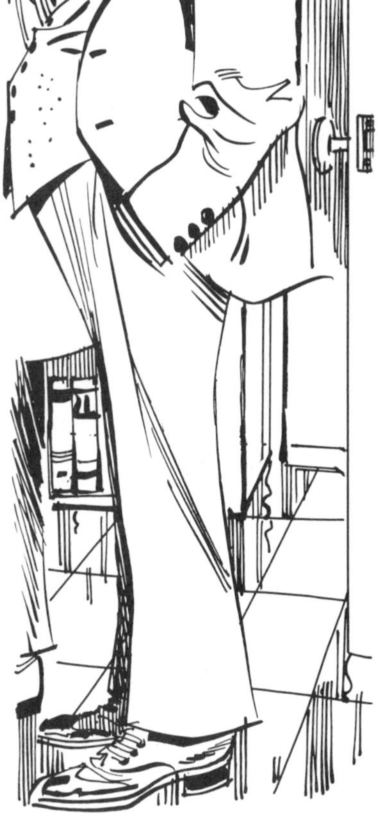

Mr. Fuller is talking with his friend, Professor Martin. They have not seen each other for a long time. They are looking at a picture of Professor Martin's family. Mr. Fuller is asking Professor Martin some questions. Professor Martin is answering.

1. Are you a professor now?
    Yes, I am.
    I'm a law professor.

2. Is this a picture of your family?
    Yes, it is.

3. Is that your brother?
    Yes, it is.
    That's Jack.

4. Is he a doctor now?
    Yes, he is.

5. Is that Mary?
    Yes, it is.
    She's a teacher.

6. Is she an English teacher?
    No, she's a science teacher.

DIALOG FOR COMPREHENSION: OLD FRIENDS TALK

Mr. Watson and Mr. Smith are still in Mr. Smith's office. They continue their conversation. Barbara is Mr. Watson's wife.

Listen to this dialog several times. Make sure you understand it. Learn the new words.

MR. SMITH	How's your family?
MR. WATSON	Barbara's fine. She's a nurse now.
MR. SMITH	And how's your daughter?
MR. WATSON	Ellie's fine, too. And Tom's in nursery school.
MR. SMITH	Tom?
MR. WATSON	Yes, he's our son. Say, is that your wife, Bill?
MR. SMITH	My wife? Where?
MR. WATSON	There. In the picture on your desk.

MR. SMITH   Oh, no! Ha, ha! I'm not married.
             That's my sister and her son.

SECRETARY   Excuse me, Mr. Smith.
             Mr. Ross is here.

NEW VOCABULARY IN LESSON 3

NOUNS	VERB	ADJECTIVES	ADVERBS
artist person	talk	best	here
brother picture		young	now
daughter school			too
desk science			
engineer sister			
English son			
law wife			
people *(pl.)*			

GRAMMAR WORDS	COMPOUNDS	NAMES
Article: an	English teacher	Family Names:
Possessive Determiner:	law professor	Martin
her	nursery school	Platte
Subject Pronouns:	science teacher	Todd
they we		Masculine Name:
Contractions:	EXPRESSIONS	Jack
we're they're		Feminine Name:
Question Word:	be married	Mary
where	Excuse me.	
Prepositions:	ha	
in of on	Oh!	
Response Word:	practice law	
no		
Negator: not		

UNIT I LESSON 3 | 21

LESSON 4

BASIC SENTENCES

Listen to these sentences. Then repeat them.

1. This is Miss Green.
2. And this is her desk.
3. Her desk is big.

4. That's Miss Long.
5. And that's her desk.
6. Her desk is small.

7. This is a telephone.
8. And this is a typewriter.

9. That's a tape recorder.
10. That's a tape.

11. This is a cassette tape recorder.
12. This is a cassette.

QUESTIONS AND ANSWERS

Listen to these questions and answers. Repeat the questions. Then repeat the answers.

1.

What's this?
　It's a telephone.

2.

What's this?
　It's a typewriter.

3.

What's this?
　It's a pen.
　It's a blue pen.

4.

What's that?
　That's a letter.
　It's a business letter.

5.

What's that over there?
　It's a radio.
　It's a portable radio.
　It's new.

6.
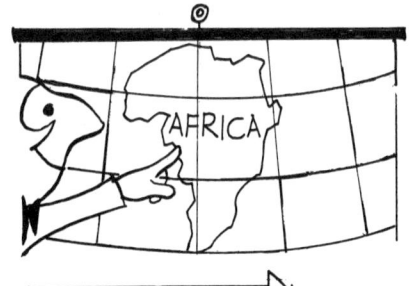
What's that on the wall?
　It's a map.
　It's a map of Africa.

UNIT 1 LESSON 4 | 23

PRONUNCIATION PRACTICE: NOUN COMPOUNDS*

Look at these two groups of words.

(1)	(2)
teacher	English teacher
English	law professor
professor	law book
book	science teacher
law	science book
science	English professor

The words in Group (1) and Group (2) are nouns. The nouns in Group (2) have two words. They are called noun compounds. In a noun compound, the first word is always spoken louder than the second word.

Repeat these noun compounds.

English professor	English teacher
law professor	science teacher
science professor	tape recorder
law book	typewriter
science book	business letter
English book	nursery school

Repeat these sentences.

That's a typewriter.	He's my English professor.
It's a business letter.	She's my science teacher.
This is a tape recorder.	That's my science book.

INTONATION

1 Question-word (Wh-) Questions and Statements

Repeat these sentences with *full markings*.

Who's that?	That's John Jones.
What's that?	It's a typewriter.

---

*Noun compounds will be listed separately in the Lesson vocabularies. Special practice with these forms is given systematically, both in the oral workbook which accompanies the text and on the tapes.

Who's that over there? That's Jim Nelson.

What's this? That's my new pen.

Repeat these sentences with *abbreviated markings*.

An arrow (↘) is used in the rest of this book to mark statements and question-word questions. The arrow is placed over the syllable that has the high pitch and the loud stress in the sentence. Syllables before this have mid pitch and syllables after it have low pitch.

Who's that? That's Bob Watson.

Who's that over there? That's Jim Nelson.

What's this? That's my tape recorder.

And what's that? That's a cassette.

2 Sentence Stress

Listen and repeat.

Very frequently in English the last word in the sentence is the word that has the high pitch and the loudest stress.

He's a good friend. They're my brother and sister.

My daughter's fine. Where's my book?

The last word is not always the loudest word. In the sentences below, the arrow is placed over the loudest word in the sentence.

That's not your book. It's my book.

That isn't Mr. Smith. It's Mrs. Smith.

How are you, Mr. Watson?

CONVERSATION PRACTICE

Listen to these questions and answers. Repeat the questions. Then repeat the answers.

1.

What's this?
   A pencil.
   It's a green pencil.

2.

And what are these?
   Red pens.
   They're red pens.

3.

What's that?
   A clock.
   It's a clock.

4.

What are those?
   Books.
   They're new books.

5.

Where are the books?
   On the table.
   They're on the table.

6.

Where's the clock?
   There.
   Over there.
   On the wall.

7.

Where are the red pens?
   There.
   They're on your desk.

8.

Where's the green pencil?
   It's on your desk, too.

9.

Where's Tom?
   He's in his room.
   He's in bed.

10.

Where's Ellie?
   She's in her room.

11.

Where's Mr. Watson?
   In his office.

12.

And where's Mr. Smith?
   He's in his office, too.

INTONATION: YES/NO QUESTIONS

Repeat these yes/no questions and answers with *full markings*.

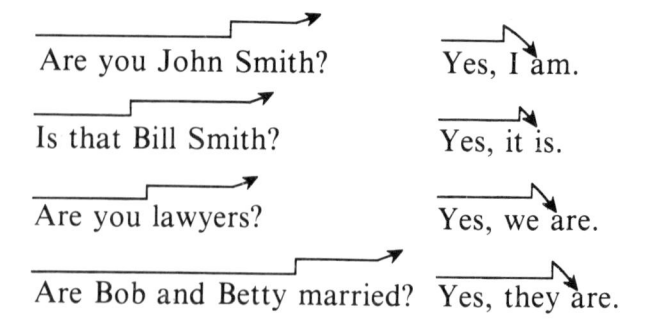

Are you John Smith?   Yes, I am.
Is that Bill Smith?   Yes, it is.
Are you lawyers?   Yes, we are.
Are Bob and Betty married?   Yes, they are.

Repeat these questions and answers with *abbreviated markings*.

In the rest of the book, the yes/no question intonation is marked with an arrow (↗) pointing up. The arrow is over the syllable with high pitch.

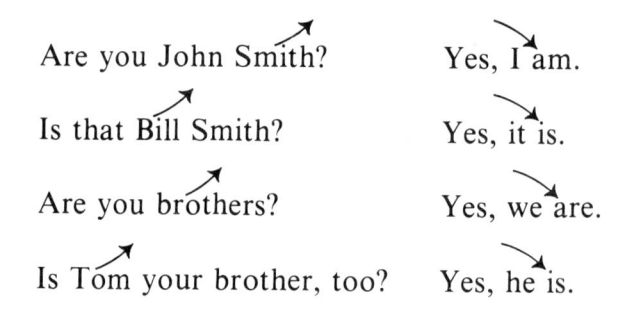

Are you John Smith?   Yes, I am.
Is that Bill Smith?   Yes, it is.
Are you brothers?   Yes, we are.
Is Tom your brother, too?   Yes, he is.

PRACTICE DRILLS AND EXERCISES*

Short Answers: Affirmative

Answer the questions with short answers.

Examples:

Are you a professor?   Yes, *I am.*
Is that your tape recorder?   Yes, *it is.*
Are those your friends?   Yes, *they are.*

---

*Only certain sentences are given intonation markings. In these cases marking is often done selectively. It is used to indicate a change in the normal stress pattern for contrast or emphasis.

1. Is Mr. Watson a scientist?   Yes, ...
2. Is Miss Green a secretary?   Yes, ...
3. Are you a student?   Yes, ...
4. Is Mr. Smith a lawyer?   Yes, ...
5. Is that your desk?   Yes, ...
6. Are those cassettes?   Yes, ...
7. Are they your friends?   Yes, ...
8. Is this your brother?   Yes, ...
9. Is Mr. Smith in?   Yes, ...
10. Is that your mother?   Yes, ...
11. Is Mr. Todd in Africa?   Yes, ...
12. Are Barbara and Jane good friends?   Yes, ...
13. Is Mary in nursery school?   Yes, ...
14. Are the pictures on his desk?   Yes, ...

LISTENING PRACTICE: THE DINNER GUEST

Mr. Smith comes to the Watsons' home for dinner. He rings the bell and Mrs. Watson answers. They have not seen each other for some time.

Listen to the conversation. Then answer the questions about it.

MR. SMITH	Barbara! It's good to see you again. How are you?
MRS. WATSON	Fine, Bill. And how are you?
MR. SMITH	Just fine. Where are Ellie and Tom?
MRS. WATSON	Tom's in bed. And Ellie's in her room. *(calls)* Ellie! Ellie! Mr. Smith is here.
ELLIE	Yes, Mother. *(Ellie comes into the room.)*
MRS. WATSON	Ellie, this is Mr. Smith. He's an old friend.
ELLIE	Hello, Mr. Smith.
MR. SMITH	Hello, Ellie. You're a big girl now! *(Mr. Watson comes in.)*
MR. WATSON	Hello, Bill. It's good to see you.
MRS. WATSON	Please come in and sit down.

NEW VOCABULARY IN LESSON 4

NOUNS				ADJECTIVES
bed	dinner	mother	room	big
business	guest	pen	table	blue
cassette	letter	pencil	telephone	green
class	map	radio	wall	red
clock				small

GRAMMAR WORDS	COMPOUNDS	EXPRESSIONS
Article: the	business letter	cassette tape recorder
Possessive Determiner: his	dinner guest	in bed
	English book	in class
Demonstrative Pronouns: these those	English professor	portable radio
	law book	
Question Word: what	science book	NAME
Contractions:	science professor	
what's where's	typewriter	Place Name: Africa

UNIT 1 LESSON 4 | 31

UNIT 2

THE PEOPLE IN UNIT 2

JAMES CARTER
(Mrs. Watson's younger brother)
Age 20
Student at the University of Chicago
Staying with the Watson family for the summer

JANE CARLSON
(new neighbor)
Age 23
Housewife
Married to Eric Carlson

IRENE LING
(neighbor and friend)
Age 28
Writer
Married to Fred Ling

LESSON 5

DIALOG: VISITORS

Mrs. Watson (Barbara) has invited her friend Mrs. Ling (Irene) to bring a new neighbor, Mrs. Carlson (Jane), to her house for tea. Mrs. Watson has not yet met Mrs. Carlson.

(knock on door)

MRS. WATSON   Hello, Irene. Please come in.

MRS. LING   Barbara Watson, this is Jane Carlson.

MRS. WATSON   How do you do?

MRS. CARLSON   It's nice to know you, Mrs. Watson.

MRS. WATSON   Oh, please call me Barbara.

MRS. LING   Jane's from Canada.

MRS. WATSON   Oh, my father's Canadian. He's from Montreal.

MRS. CARLSON   I'm from there, too!

MRS. LING   Well, isn't that interesting!

PRACTICE DRILLS AND EXERCISES

1   Making Introductions (1)

Listen and repeat.

MR. WATSON INTRODUCES MR. JONES TO MR. SMITH.

MR. WATSON   Mr. Smith, this is Mr. Jones.
Mr. Jones, Mr. Smith.

MR. LONG INTRODUCES MR. JONES TO MRS. WATSON.

MR. LONG   Mrs. Watson, this is Mr. Jones.
Mr. Jones, Mrs. Watson.

MRS. LING INTRODUCES MRS. JANE CARLSON TO MRS. BARBARA WATSON.

MRS. LING   Barbara, this is Jane Carlson.
Jane, Barbara.

2 Making Introductions (2)

Repeat these introductions.

I'd like you to meet Miss Green.
I want you to know Mr. Wilson.
I want you to meet Jim Carter.
I'd like you to meet my sister Ann.
I want you to meet Jane Carlson.

Substitute the names.

I'd like you to meet *Miss Foster.*
I'd like you to meet *my brother Bill.* (my brother Bill)
.... (Mr. Carlson)
.... (Tom Carter)
.... (my wife Jane)

3 Acknowledging Introductions

Repeat after Speaker B.

SPEAKER A		SPEAKER B
1. Mr. Jones, this is Mr. Smith.	MR. JONES	How do you do?
2. Mr. Ross, Mr. Long.	MR. ROSS	I'm glad to know you.
3. Mrs. Watson, this is Mr. Ross.	MRS. WATSON	How do you do, Mr. Ross?
4. Barbara, I'd like you to meet Jane.	BARBARA	It's nice to know you.
5. Helen, I want you to know Tom.	HELEN	I'm glad to meet you.
6. I'd like you to meet Mr. Carlson.	MR. WATSON	How do you do?

4 Introducing People

Listen and repeat.

MRS. LING   Barbara Watson, I want you to know Jane Carlson. Jane, Barbara.

MRS. WATSON   It's nice to meet you, Jane.

MRS. CARLSON   I'm glad to know you.

MR. WATSON	Mr. Smith, this is Mr. Wilson. Mr. Wilson, Mr. Smith.
MR. SMITH	How do you do?
MR. WILSON	I'm glad to know you.
MR. BROWN	Dr. Nelson, I'd like you to meet Mr. Porter. Mr. Porter, Dr. Nelson.
DR. NELSON	How do you do?
MR. PORTER	How do you do?
TOM SMITH	Marge, this is Steve. Steve, this is Marge.
MARGE	I'm glad to know you.
STEVE	I'm glad to know you.
MR. SHAW	Mr. Carlson, I'd like you to meet Bob.
MR. CARLSON	I'm glad to know you, Bob.
BOB	How do you do, Mr. Carlson?

BASIC SENTENCES

Listen to these sentences. Then repeat them.

1. My name's Robert Nelson.
2. My first name's Robert.
3. My last name's Nelson.
4. I'm a doctor.
5. I'm Dr. Nelson.

6. That's my sister.
7. Her name's Dorothy Nelson.
8. Her first name's Dorothy.
9. Her last name's Nelson.

10. That man's Mr. Wood.
11. His last name's Wood.
12. His first name's Owen.
13. His middle name is Thomas.
14. His full name's Owen Thomas Wood.

QUESTIONS AND ANSWERS

Listen to these questions and answers. Repeat the questions. Then repeat the answers.

1. MR. WOOD AND MR. JOHNSON

    Excuse me, are you Mr. Taylor?
    No, I'm not.
    My name's Johnson.

2. MR. TAYLOR AND MR. TODD

    Is that Fred Johnson over there?
    No, it's not.
    That's his brother.

3. MR. GREEN AND MR. WOOD

    Is Owen your last name?
    No, it's not.
    Owen's my first name.

4. MR. WATSON AND MR. LING

Is Eric Carlson an engineer?
No, he's not.
He's a chemist.

5. TOM NELSON AND MARGE GREEN

Are you Miss Green?
Yes, I am.
Is your first name Mary?
No, it's Marge.
Oh, I'm sorry.

QUESTIONS TO ANSWER

Look at the picture and answer the questions.

(a) DOCTOR

ROBERT LONG NELSON

(b) ENGINEER

JAMES BROWN TAYLOR

(c) ARTIST

(MRS.) MARY ANN WOOD

Who is this man?
What's his first name?
What's his last name?
What's his full name?
Is he an engineer?

Is this Mr. Taylor?
Is this his picture?
Is the picture on the wall?
What's his first name?
What's his last name?

Who is this woman?
Is she an artist?
What's her last name?
What's her middle name?
Is she married?

NEW VOCABULARY IN LESSON 5

NOUN	VERBS		ADJECTIVES		
chemist	call	like	Canadian	glad	last
	do	meet	first	interesting	sorry
	know	want			

GRAMMAR WORDS

Demonstrative Determiner: this
Preposition: from
Contraction: isn't

EXPRESSIONS

full name
How do you do?
I'd like...
Well, ...
Call me (Barbara).
middle name

TITLE & NAMES

Title: Dr./Doctor
Family Names:
    Foster   Taylor   Wood
    Porter   Wilson
Masculine Names:
    Fred   Steve
    Owen   Thomas
Feminine Names:
    Ann   Helen   Marge
    Dorothy   Irene
Place Names:
    Canada   Montreal

LESSON 6

DIALOG: GETTING ACQUAINTED

Mrs. Watson invites Mrs. Ling and Mrs. Carlson into the living room. They continue their conversation. Jim Carter is Mrs. Watson's younger brother. (Her name was Carter before she married Mr. Watson.) Ellie is the daughter of Mr. and Mrs. Watson.

MRS. LING	Is Jim home?
MRS. WATSON	No, he isn't. He's out with Ellie.
MRS. CARLSON	Is Jim your husband?
MRS. WATSON	No, he's my brother. He's here for the summer.
MRS. LING	Barbara's husband is a scientist.
MRS. CARLSON	My husband is, too!
MRS. LING	Well, isn't that interesting!

PRACTICE DRILLS AND EXERCISES (1)

1 BE: Forming Yes/No Questions

Take the part of Speaker A. Form yes/no questions.

	SPEAKER A	SPEAKER B
STATEMENT OF FACT	YES/NO QUESTION	AFFIRMATIVE SHORT ANSWER
1. MRS. ROSS IS HERE.	*Is Mrs. Ross here?*	Yes, she is.
2. THEY'RE ENGINEERS.	*Are they engineers?*	Yes, they are.
3. THAT'S BOB.	*Is that Bob?*	Yes, it is.
4. HE'S MR. SMITH.	...................?	Yes, he is.
5. BOB'S HER HUSBAND.	...................?	Yes, he is.
6. HIS FIRST NAME IS JOHN.	...................?	Yes, it is.
7. SHE'S A TYPIST.	...................?	Yes, she is.
8. THAT'S A MAP.	...................?	Yes, it is.
9. MR. SMITH IS IN.	...................?	Yes, he is.
10. THEY'RE STUDENTS.	...................?	Yes, they are.

2 BE: Negative Short Answers

Take the part of Speaker B. Give negative short answers.

	SPEAKER A	SPEAKER B
	YES/NO QUESTION	NEGATIVE SHORT ANSWER
1.	Is Mr. Smith in?	*No, he's not.*
2.	Are they professors?	*No, they're not.*
3.	Are you Mr. Ross?	*No, I'm not.*
4.	Is this your office?	*No, it's not.*
5.	Is Mrs. Watson a doctor?	....
6.	Is Jones your first name?	....
7.	Am I an artist?	....
8.	Are they brother and sister?	....

9. Are you a scientist? ....
10. Are we professors? ....
11. Is that your son? ....
12. Are you here for the summer? ....

3 Negative Contractions: *isn't/aren't*

Repeat the sentences.

He's not married. He isn't married.
It's not here. It isn't here.
We're not friends. We aren't friends.
They're not sisters. They aren't sisters.
John's not my brother. John isn't my brother.
I'm not a doctor.

Complete the sentences. Use *isn't* or *aren't*.

1. He's not here.
   He isn't here.

2. Mary's not my sister.
   Mary isn't my sister.

3. You're not old.
   ...... old.

4. She's not a nurse.
   ...... a nurse.

5. The letter's not here.
   ...... here.

6. They're not friends.
   ...... friends.

7. It's not new.
   ...... new.

8. That's not my clock.
   ...... my clock.

9. We're not brothers.
   ...... brothers.

10. You're not in the picture.
    ...... in the picture.

4 Yes/No Questions and Answers

Answer the questions with short answers. Take the part of Student B. Use *isn't* or *aren't*.

STUDENT A
(Use *is* or *are*)

1. *Are* they your friends?
2. *Is* she your sister?
3. ...... he a teacher?

STUDENT B
(Use *isn't* or *aren't*)

No, they *aren't*. ....
No, she *isn't*. ......
No, he ....

UNIT 2 LESSON 6 | 41

4. ...... they visitors?   No, they ....
5. ...... her first name Mary?   No, it ....
6. ...... they dentists?   No, they ....
7. ...... that a good chair?   No, it ....
8. ...... she his daughter?   No, she ....
9. ...... Mary and Kathy nurses?   No, they ....
10. ...... Jim his middle name?   No, it ....
11. ...... they good friends?   No, they ....
12. ...... Mr. Watson a dentist?   No, he ....
13. ...... she a visitor?   No, she ....
14. ...... that your desk?   No, it ....
15. ...... Mr. Watson from Canada?   No, he ....
16. ...... those your maps?   No, they ....
17. ...... your brother here?   No, he ....
18. ...... Jim and Bob in class?   No, they ....
19. ...... this my letter?   No, it ....
20. ...... the boys here?   No, they ....

READING: MRS. WATSON AND HER FAMILY

I'm Mrs. Watson. My first name is Barbara. I'm a nurse and I work in a hospital. I'm married to Robert Watson. He's a scientist.

My husband and I live in Wisconsin. That's one of the states in the United States. We live in a house. Our house isn't new and it isn't large. But we like it very much.

We have one daughter. Her name's Ellie. Her room is upstairs. It isn't big, but it's very nice. We also have a young son. His name's Tom.

PRACTICE DRILLS AND EXERCISES (2)

1 Negative Statements and Conjunction

Repeat these sentences.

1. We aren't doctors.
   We aren't dentists.
   　　We aren't doctors and we aren't dentists.
   　　We're professors.

2. They aren't teachers.
   They aren't students.
   　　They aren't teachers and they aren't students.
   　　They're visitors.

3. You're not from Thailand.
   You're not from Australia.
   　　You're not from Thailand and you're not from Australia.
   　　You're from Japan.

4. They aren't from Canada.
   They aren't from England.
   　　They aren't from Canada and they aren't from England.
   　　They're from the United States.

2 Negative and Affirmative Statements

Repeat these sentences.

He isn't a doctor. He's a lawyer.
She isn't a teacher. She's a nurse.
This isn't a pen. It's a pencil.
Bill isn't a student. He's a teacher.
Barbara isn't a typist. She's a nurse.

Construct sentences. Use the contraction *isn't*.

MR. SMITH IS A LAWYER.

1. Is Mr. Smith a doctor?
   No, he *isn't a doctor. He's a lawyer.*

MR. WATSON IS A SCIENTIST.

2. Is Mr. Watson a lawyer?
   No, he *isn't a lawyer. He's a scientist.*

MRS. WATSON IS A NURSE.

3. Is Mrs. Watson a secretary?
   No, she ....

MR. CARLSON IS A CHEMIST.

4. Is Mr. Carlson a dentist?
   No, he ....

THIS IS A PICTURE.

5. Is this a map?

   No, it ....

MISS GREEN IS A SECRETARY.

6. Is Miss Green a teacher?

   No, she ....

NEW VOCABULARY IN LESSON 6

NOUNS	VERBS	ADJECTIVE	ADVERBS
chair state hospital summer husband	have live work	large	also home out upstairs

GRAMMAR WORDS	EXPRESSIONS	NUMBER & NAMES

Contraction: aren't
Prepositions:
  for to with
Possessive Determiner:
  our
	get acquainted
	for the summer
	very much
		Number: one
		Place Names:
		  Australia Thailand
		  England United States
		  Japan Wisconsin

LESSON 7

QUESTIONS AND ANSWERS

Listen to these questions and answers. Repeat the questions. Then repeat the answers.

1.

What's that?
   It's a letter from Tom.

Who's Tom?
   He's my brother.

2.

What are those?
   They're birthday cards.
   They're from Irene and Jane.

Who are Irene and Jane?
   They're my neighbors.

3.

What's that?
   It's a picture of Mr. Chang.

Who's Mr. Chang?
   He's president of Orient Airlines.

4.

What's that?
   It's a gift from Cathy.

Who's Cathy?
   She's my little sister.

PRACTICE DRILLS AND EXERCISES (1)

1 Identifying Things: Question-word (Wh-) Questions with *What*

Repeat the questions after Speaker A.

STATEMENT OF FACT	SPEAKER A WH- QUESTION	SPEAKER B ANSWER
1. THAT'S A MAP.	What's that?	It's a map.
2. THIS IS A LETTER FROM TOM.	What's this?	It's a letter from Tom.
3. THESE ARE PICTURES.	What are these?	They're pictures.
4. THOSE ARE TEXTBOOKS.	What are those?	They're textbooks.

Take the part of Speaker A. Form wh- questions.

STATEMENT OF FACT	SPEAKER A WH- QUESTION	SPEAKER B ANSWER
1. THAT'S A BUSINESS LETTER.	.............?	It's a business letter.
2. THOSE ARE MAPS.	.............?	They're maps.
3. THIS IS A NEW BOOK.	.............?	It's a new book.
4. THOSE ARE TABLES.	.............?	They're tables.

Take the part of Speaker B. Begin your answer with *it's* or *they're*.

STATEMENT OF FACT	SPEAKER A WH- QUESTION	SPEAKER B ANSWER
1. THIS IS A CASSETTE.	What's this?	....
2. THESE ARE TAPES.	What are these?	....
3. THAT'S A TAPE RECORDER.	What's that?	....
4. THOSE ARE PENS.	What are those?	....

UNIT 2 LESSON 7 | 47

2 Identifying People: Question-word (Wh-) Questions with *Who*

Form questions using *who*.

STATEMENT OF FACT	SPEAKER A WH- QUESTION	SPEAKER B ANSWER
1. THAT'S MY BROTHER.	*Who's that?*	That's my brother.
2. THOSE MEN ARE JIM AND BILL.	*Who are those men?*	They're Jim and Bill.
3. CATHY'S MY LITTLE SISTER.	*Who's Cathy?*	She's my little sister.
4. THAT MAN'S DR. BLACK.	............?	That's Dr. Black.
5. JANE'S HIS DAUGHTER.	............?	She's his daughter.
6. THAT WOMAN IS MRS. CARLSON.	............?	It's Mrs. Carlson.
7. THAT LITTLE BOY IS TOM.	............?	It's Tom.
8. THAT'S MR. SMITH.	............?	It's Mr. Smith.

3 Identifying People: Question-word (Wh-) Questions with *Who*

Complete the sentences.

STATEMENT OF FACT	SPEAKER A WH- QUESTION	SPEAKER B ANSWER
1. THAT'S MY SISTER.	*Who's that?*	That's my sister.
2. THAT LITTLE GIRL IS JANE.	............?	That's Jane.
3. THOSE MEN ARE TOM AND FRED.	............?	They're Tom and Fred.
4. BILL'S HIS SON.	............?	He's his son.
5. THAT NURSE IS MISS BLACK.	............?	That's Miss Black.
6. THAT BOY OVER THERE IS BOB.	............?	....
7. THAT MAN'S HER HUSBAND.	............?	....
8. THOSE PEOPLE ARE VISITORS.	............?	....
9. JIMMY'S MY LITTLE BROTHER.	............?	....

10. . . . . Who are those men? They're visitors.
11. . . . . Who is this girl? This is my daughter.
12. . . . . Who are those boys? They're my brothers.
13. . . . . Who is that lady? That's Mrs. Carlson.

DIALOG: VISITING

Mrs. Ling and Mrs. Carlson are still at Mrs. Watson's house. Mrs. Watson and Mrs. Carlson are talking.

MRS. WATSON	What does your husband do?
MRS. CARLSON	He's a chemist.
MRS. WATSON	Is he at the university?
MRS. CARLSON	No, he isn't. He's with the Lamar Lumber Company.
MRS. WATSON	Oh, my uncle's an accountant there. It's a very big company!
MRS. CARLSON	Yes, it certainly is. Is your husband a professor?
MRS. WATSON	No, he's with the government. He's a biologist.

UNIT 2 LESSON 7 | 49

PRACTICE DRILLS AND EXERCISES (2)

1 Asking about Occupations

(What's his occupation? = What is he? = What does he do?)

Substitute the occupations. Use *he* or *she* as appropriate.

	TEACHER	STUDENT
1.	What's his occupation?	He's *an accountant.*
2.	What's her occupation?	She's *a nurse.* (a nurse)
3.	What is Tom?	............(an engineer)
4.	What is Mrs. Larson?	............(a professor)
5.	What is Mr. Jones?	............(a lawyer)
6.	What's Mr. Carlson?	............(a chemist)
7.	What's her occupation?	............(a biologist)
8.	What's Miss Long?	............(a typist)

Listen to these conversational exchanges.

1. What does Mr. Smith do?
   He's a lawyer.

2. What's your occupation?
   I'm a professor.

3. What's Mr. Watson?
   He's a biologist.

4. What do Fred and Tom do?
   They're lawyers.

5. Mr. Watson isn't a lawyer.
   What is he?
   He's a scientist.

6. Miss Long isn't a secretary.
   What is she?
   She's a typist.

7. I'm not a doctor.
   What are you?
   I'm a professor.

50| UNIT 2 LESSON 7

Repeat the questions.

TEACHER	STUDENT
1. What do you do?	STUDENT 1 I'm a lawyer.
2. What do you do?	STUDENT 2 I'm a biologist.
3. And what do you do?	STUDENT 3 I'm a chemist.
4. Mr. Smith, what do you do?	STUDENT 4 I'm a doctor.

2 Asking about Occupations

Take the part of the student.

TEACHER	STUDENT
1. What does Mr. Watson do? *(biologist)*	*He's a biologist.*
2. What's Miss Green? *(secretary)*	*She's a secretary.*
3. What's your occupation? *(professor)*	*I'm a professor.*
4. What's my occupation? *(teacher)*	....
5. What does Mr. Smith do? *(lawyer)*	....
6. What are Jim and Ted? *(students)*	....
7. What are you? *(professor)*	....
8. What's Mr. Jones? *(engineer)*	....
9. What does Miss Platte do? *(artist)*	....
10. What do Miss Long and Mrs. Black do? *(typists)*	....
11. What's Dr. Morton? *(law professor)*	....
12. What's his occupation? *(accountant)*	....

NEW VOCABULARY IN LESSON 7

NOUNS			ADJECTIVE	ADVERB
accountant	gift	occupation	little	certainly
biologist	government	president		
card	lumber	uncle		
company	neighbor	university		

GRAMMAR WORDS	COMPOUNDS	NAMES

Auxiliary Verbs:
   do   does
Preposition: at
Demonstrative Determiner:
   those
	airline
	birthday
	birthday card
	lumber company
	textbook
		Family Names:
		   Black Larson
		   Chang Morton
		Feminine Name: Cathy
		Company Names:
		   Lamar Lumber Company
		   Orient Airlines

LESSON 8

CONVERSATION PRACTICE

Listen to these conversations. Then repeat.

BILL   Isn't this your pen?

BOB   Yes, it is.
Thank you.

JIM   Who's that lady?

BOB   Isn't that Irene Ling?

JIM   Yes, you're right. It is.

JOHN   Aren't you Tom Wheeler?

BILL   No, I'm not.
My name's Bill Johnson.

BETTY   Isn't Miss Lee from Korea?

MARGE   Yes, but she isn't Korean.
She's Chinese.

TOM   Aren't you Eric Carlson from Wisconsin?

ERIC   I'm Eric Carlson.
But I'm from Minnesota.

TOM   Oh, yes, I remember now.
I'm Tom Evers.

ERIC   Well, imagine that!
It's good to see you again, Tom.

JIM Ed, come here for a minute.

ED All right. What is it?

JIM Look. Isn't that your sister?

ED Where?

JIM Over there.

ED No, that's not Mary. It's Becky.

PRACTICE DRILLS AND EXERCISES (1)

1 Negative Questions: Intonation Practice

Repeat these questions.

(a)

Isn't that *Tom Wilson?*
Isn't that *your sister?*
Isn't that *Mr. Chang?*
Isn't that *Kathleen Nelson?*
Isn't that *your brother?*

(b)

Isn't this *your house?*
Isn't this *your pen?*
Isn't this *my tape?*
Isn't this *your office?*
Isn't this *our radio?*

2 Negative Questions: Short Answers

Speaker A: Fill the blanks with *isn't* or *aren't*.
Speaker B: Reply with short answers.

	SPEAKER A	SPEAKER B
1.	*Aren't* we early?	Yes, *we are.*
2.	*Isn't* this your pen?	No, *it isn't.*
3.	*Aren't* John and Ted engineers?	Yes, *they are.*
4.	...... she your sister?	Yes, ...
5.	...... you and Maria Spanish?	Yes, ...
6.	...... your first name Bill?	No, ...
7.	...... you Tom Smith?	Yes, ...
8.	...... Owen your last name?	No, ...

9. ...... Irene your neighbor?   Yes, ...
10. ...... they your children?   No, ...
11. ...... Mr. Chang here?   No, ...
12. ...... you from Japan?   Yes, ...
13. ...... that your house?   Yes, ...
14. ...... Ed and Ella married?   No, ...
15. ...... Mr. Wheeler an accountant? Yes, ...

3 Irregular Noun Plurals (New Vocabulary)

Repeat these sentences.

1. Bob's a businessman.
   I'm a businessman, too.
       We're businessmen.

2. My father's a tall man.
   My brother's a tall man, too.
       They're tall men.

3. My mother's a short woman.
   Her sister's a short woman, too.
       They're short women.

4. His brother's a policeman.
   His son's a policeman, too.
       They're policemen.

5. Mary's just a child.
   Eric's a young child, too.
       They're just young children.

6. His father's a fireman.
   His brother's a fireman, too.
       They're firemen.

Say the last sentence. Fill in the blank.

1. Mr. Oda's a Japanese businessman.
   Mr. Okayama's a Japanese businessman, too.
   They're Japanese *businessmen.*

2. Mr. Carlson's a Swedish scientist.
   Mr. Olson's a Swedish scientist, too.
   They're Swedish ....

3. Tom's a small child.
   Mary's a small child, too.
   They're small ....

4. Mrs. Ling's a nice woman.
   Mrs. Carlson's a nice woman, too.
   They're nice ....

5. Jim Carter's a young man.
   Mr. Nelson's a young man, too.
   They're young ....

6. He's a good businessman.
   I'm a good businessman, too.
   We're good ....

LISTENING PRACTICE: INTRODUCING JIM

Mrs. Ling and Mrs. Carlson are still at Mrs. Watson's house talking. Ellie and Jim Carter (Mrs. Watson's younger brother) come home as they are talking.

MRS. WATSON	Oh, there are Jim and Ellie.
MRS. CARLSON	Is Jim your brother?
MRS. WATSON	Yes, he is. *(calls)* Oh . . . Jim! Ellie!
JIM CARTER	Yes?
MRS. WATSON	Please come here for a minute.
JIM CARTER	All right.
ELLIE	Okay, Mother.
	(Jim and Ellie come in)
MRS. WATSON	Mrs. Carlson, this is Jim. Mrs. Carlson is our new neighbor.
JIM CARTER	How do you do, Mrs. Carlson?
MRS. CARLSON	I'm glad to know you, Jim.
MRS. WATSON	And this is our daughter, Ellie.
ELLIE	How do you do, Mrs. Carlson?
MRS. CARLSON	I'm glad to know you, Ellie.
MRS. WATSON	And you know Mrs. Ling.
JIM CARTER	Yes. Nice to see you again.
MRS. WATSON	Jim's a university student.
MRS. CARLSON	Oh . . . Where?
JIM CARTER	At the University of Chicago. Where are you from, Mrs. Carlson?
MRS. CARLSON	I'm from Canada. But my husband's from Minnesota.

PRACTICE DRILLS AND EXERCISES (2)

1 First Names: Full Forms and Short Forms

Study these first names and repeat them.

MASCULINE		FEMININE	
FULL FORM	SHORT FORM	FULL FORM	SHORT FORM
Robert	Bob	Kathleen	Kathy
William	Bill	Eleanor	Ellie
James	Jim	Barbara	Barb
Thomas	Tom	Elizabeth	Betty
Steven	Steve	Margaret	Marge
Edwin	Ed	Dorothy	Dot
Frederick	Fred	Rebecca	Becky
Eric	*(No short form)*	Mary	*(No short form)*
Owen	*(No short form)*	Jane	*(No short form)*
Roy	*(No short form)*	Irene	*(No short form)*

Listen to these conversational exchanges.

ROBERT WATSON	Hello, Bill. How are you?
WILLIAM JONES	Fine, Bob. How are you?
ELIZABETH NELSON	Here's your book, Barb.
BARBARA WATSON	Oh, thanks, Betty.
REBECCA BLACK	Hello, Dot.
DOROTHY WILSON	Hi, Becky.
STEVEN NELSON	Here's your pen, Tom.
THOMAS GREEN	Thanks, Steve.

2 First Names: Short Forms

Take the part of Mr. Ross in these conversations. Use short forms of the personal names.

FREDERICK GREEN	Hello, Bob.
ROBERT ROSS	Hello, ... How are you?
WILLIAM JONES	Hi, Bob.
ROBERT ROSS	Hello, ...
REBECCA BLACK	Is Jane home, Bob?
ROBERT ROSS	Yes, come in . . . . . .
KATHLEEN WHEELER	Isn't Barb here?
ROBERT ROSS	No, she isn't . . . . . . She's at the hospital.
STEVEN NELSON	Isn't this your letter?
ROBERT ROSS	Yes, thanks . . . . . .
JAMES WOOD	Come in, Bob.
ROBERT ROSS	Thanks . . . . . . Say, this is a nice office!

3 Making an Interested Comment by Using *isn't/aren't* with Falling Intonation

(Isn't that interesting! = That's very interesting!)

Repeat.

Isn't that interesting!
Aren't you nice!

Isn't she a short woman!
Isn't he tall!

Repeat after Speaker B.

	SPEAKER A	SPEAKER B
1.	That's Betty over there.	My, isn't she pretty!
2.	My father's from Montreal.	Well, isn't that interesting!
3.	This is a gift for you.	Well, aren't you nice!
4.	My friend's a scientist.	Well, isn't that interesting!
5.	That's Jim over there.	My, isn't he tall!

4 Question-word (Wh-) Questions with *Who* and *What*

Take the part of Speaker B.

A   This isn't a pen.

B   *What is it?*

A   *It's a pencil.*

A   That isn't Bob.

B   *Who is it?*

A   *It's Tom.*

A Tom and Ted aren't doctors.

B *What are they?*

A *They're lawyers.*

A That isn't Tom.

B ....?

A ....

A That isn't a tape recorder.

B ....?

A ....

6

Chemist

A Eric isn't a biologist.
B ....?
A ....

7

Mary

A That isn't Barbara.
B ....?
A ....

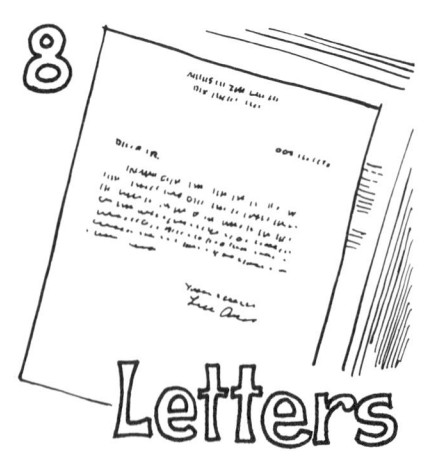

8

Letters

A These aren't birthday cards.
B ....?
A ....

NEW VOCABULARY IN LESSON 8

NOUNS		VERBS	ADJECTIVES		
child	men	imagine	Chinese	pretty	Swedish
children *(pl.)*	minute	look	early	right	tall
lady	women	remember	Japanese	short	
		introduce	Korean	Spanish	

EXPRESSIONS	NAMES
All right.　　Okay.	Family Names:
Hi!	Evers　　Oda　　Olson
Imagine that!	Lee　　Okayama　Wheeler
My!	Ling
	Masculine Names:
COMPOUNDS	Ed　　Ted
	Feminine Names:
businessman	Barb　　Dot　　Kathleen
businessmen *(pl.)*	Becky　　Ella　　Maria
fireman	Place Names:
firemen *(pl.)*	Chicago　Korea　Minnesota
policeman	School Name:
policemen *(pl.)*	University of Chicago

UNIT 3

THE PEOPLE IN UNIT 3

RODNEY HILL WATSON
(brother of Robert Watson)
Age 39
Economist
Lives in Denver, Colorado

ERIC CARLSON
(new neighbor)
Age 24
Chemist
Husband of Jane Carlson

LESSON 9

DIALOG: TALKING ABOUT THE CARLSONS

Mr. and Mrs. Watson are home on a Tuesday evening.

MRS. WATSON	The Carlsons are coming to dinner Saturday. The Lings are coming, too.
MR. WATSON	Oh, fine. Aren't the Carlsons our new neighbors?
MRS. WATSON	Yes, Jane was here this afternoon.
MR. WATSON	What's her husband's first name?
MRS. WATSON	Eric, I believe. Jane was born in Montreal.
MR. WATSON	Wasn't your father born there?
MRS. WATSON	Yes, he was.
MR. WATSON	Well, imagine that!

The Conversation Continues

MR. WATSON	How old are the Carlsons?
MRS. WATSON	Oh, they're very young.
MR. WATSON	Twenty?
MRS. WATSON	Oh, twenty-three... maybe twenty-four.
MR. WATSON	They *are* young! You say he's a scientist?
MRS. WATSON	Yes, he's a chemist.
MR. WATSON	At the university?
MRS. WATSON	No, he's with the Lamar Lumber Company.

PRACTICE DRILLS AND EXERCISES (1)

1 BE: Past Tense Forms *was/were*

Repeat these sentences.

I was here yesterday.
I was in the office all day.

Mr. Long and I were early.
We were here at eight o'clock.

You were late today.
You were late yesterday, too.

Jane was here last week.
She was here on Tuesday.

Substitute the subject forms.

I was very busy yesterday.
Bill was very busy yesterday. *(Bill)*
.... *(Miss Watson)*
.... *(Your mother)*
.... *(My secretary)*

We were quite late this morning.
Jane and Betty were quite late this morning. *(Jane and Betty)*
.... *(You)*
.... *(They)*
.... *(You and I)*

BASIC SENTENCES

Listen to these sentences. Then repeat them.

Miss Green works in Mr. Smith's law office. She's talking about coming to work early.

1. It's only eight o'clock!
2. I'm early today.
3. I was early yesterday, too.
4. Mr. Long's here.
5. He's usually on time.
6. But yesterday he was late.
7. He was an hour late!

8. Mr. Smith isn't in.
9. He was sick yesterday.
10. Oh, here's Mr. Smith now!
11. Good morning, Mr. Smith.
12. I hope you're feeling better.

PRACTICE DRILLS AND EXERCISES (2)

1 Cardinal Numbers: One to Twenty

Study these numbers and listen to them.

CARDINAL NUMBERS 1-20

1	one	6	six	11	eleven	16	sixteen
2	two	7	seven	12	twelve	17	seventeen
3	three	8	eight	13	thirteen	18	eighteen
4	four	9	nine	14	fourteen	19	nineteen
5	five	10	ten	15	fifteen	20	twenty

Count with slow deliberate counting intonation.

one   two   three   four   five
one   two   three   four   five

five   four   three   two   one

Count with normal counting intonation.

This arrow (→) represents the voice rising in pitch from the mid level. It contrasts with the voice rising from the high level (↗) as in yes/no questions.

one   two   three   four   five
one   two   three   four   five

Count deliberately.

six   seven   eight   nine   ten
ten   nine   eight   seven   six

UNIT 3 LESSON 9 | 67

Count with normal counting intonation.

six	seven	eight	nine	ten
six	seven	eight	nine	ten

Repeat these sequences.

1 2 3 4 5
1 2 3 4 5

6 7 8 9 10
6 7 8 9 10

Count from one to ten, and from ten to one.

1 2 3 4 5 6 7 8 9 10
10 9 8 7 6 5 4 3 2 1

2 Using Numbers for Enumeration and Designation

Enumeration

Substitute the nouns.

TEACHER	STUDENT
(1) I have two boys.	I have two boys.
(girls)	I have three girls.
(watches)	....
(children)	....
(tapes)	....
(birthday cards)	....
(2) Three pens were on the chair.	Three pens were on the chair.
(clocks/table)	Four clocks were on the table.
(letters/desk)	....
(pictures of Dr. Long/wall)	....
(maps of England/wall)	....

(3) We have two sons.   *We have two sons and they have three daughters.*
    (daughters)

We have three radios.   *We have three radios and they have four tape recorders.*
    (tape recorders)

We have four desks.
    (tables)

We have eight cards.
    (letters)

We have nine tapes.
    (books)

Designation

Combine each group of sentences into one sentence.

TEACHER	STUDENT
(1) Repeat Dialog 1. Repeat Dialog 2.	*Repeat Dialogs 1 and 2.*
Study page 4. Study page 5.	*Study pages 4 and 5.*
Repeat Practice 7. Repeat Practice 8. Repeat Practice 9.	*Repeat Practices 7, 8 and 9.*
Study sentence 1. Study sentence 2.	
Repeat question 6. Repeat question 7.	
Study page 8. Study page 9. Study page 10.	

(2) This is Practice 4.   *Where's Practice 5?* ....
   This is Tape 5.   *Where's Tape 6?* ....
   This is Tape Number 6.
   ....
   This is page 7.
   ....
   This is Cassette Number 8.
   ....
   This is Lesson 9.
   ....

3 Practice with Numbers Eleven to Twenty

Repeat with slow counting intonation.

eleven	twelve	thirteen	fourteen	fifteen
eleven	twelve	thirteen	fourteen	fifteen
fifteen	fourteen	thirteen	twelve	eleven

Repeat using normal counting intonation.

| eleven | twelve | thirteen | fourteen | fifteen |
| eleven | twelve | thirteen | fourteen | fifteen |

Repeat.

| sixteen | seventeen | eighteen | nineteen | twenty |
| twenty | nineteen | eighteen | seventeen | sixteen |

Repeat. Follow the intonation markings.

| sixteen | seventeen | eighteen | nineteen | twenty |
| sixteen | seventeen | eighteen | nineteen | twenty |

Repeat.

11 12 13 14 15 16 17 18 19 20

Count from eleven to twenty.

11 12 13 14 15 16 17 18 19 20
11 12 13 14 15 16 17 18 19 20

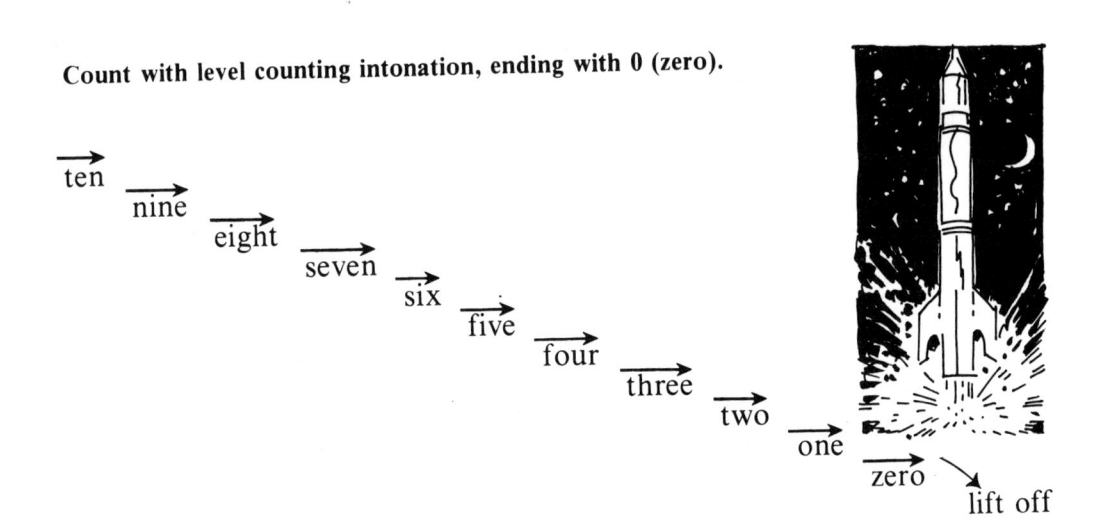

Count with level counting intonation, ending with 0 (zero).

→ten
→nine
→eight
→seven
→six
→five
→four
→three
→two
→one
→zero ↘ lift off

NEW VOCABULARY IN LESSON 9

NOUNS	VERBS	ADJECTIVES	ADVERBS
afternoon practice	BE: was, were	better	maybe
conversation question	believe	busy	o'clock
dialog Saturday	continue	late	only
hour Tuesday	feel	sick	today
lesson watch	hope		usually
number week	say		yesterday
page	study		

GRAMMAR WORDS	EXPRESSIONS	CARDINAL NUMBERS
Question Word: how old	all day	zero, one, two, three,
Prepositions:	an hour late	four, five, six, seven,
at (+ time word)	are coming	eight, nine, ten, eleven,
on (+ time word)	be born	twelve, thirteen, fourteen,
Intensifier: quite	eight o'clock	fifteen, sixteen, seventeen,
	last week	eighteen, nineteen, twenty,
NAME	lift off	(twenty-three, twenty-four)
Place Name:	on time	
Denver, Colorado		

LESSON 10

CONVERSATION PRACTICE: SIX CONVERSATIONS

Listen to these conversations. Then repeat.

MR. KING	What's your nationality?
MR. ODA	I'm Japanese.
	I was born in Tokyo.

MR. ODA	Were you born in the United States?
MR. PEREZ	Yes, I was.
	I was born in New York.
MR. ODA	In New York City?
MR. PEREZ	Yes.

MR. LEE	Miss Yang isn't Korean.
MR. LONG	What is she?
MR. LEE	She's Chinese.

MR. CARLSON	Did your mother come yesterday?
MR. PENNY	Yes, she did.
MR. CARLSON	Did your sister come, too?
MR. PENNY	No, she stayed in Denver.

MRS. CLARK	Did Dr. Black and his wife stay in that hotel?
MRS. BROWN	No, they didn't.
MRS. CLARK	Where did they stay?
MRS. BROWN	I don't know.

MR. LONG How old's your daughter?

MR. WATSON She's ten.
She was ten last week.
Her birthday was last Tuesday.

PRACTICE DRILLS AND EXERCISES

1   Conjoining with *but*

Repeat. (affirmative sentence/negative sentence)

1. He's here today.
   He wasn't here yesterday.
   He's here today, but he wasn't here yesterday.

2. We're good friends now.
   We weren't good friends last year.
   We're good friends now, but we weren't good friends last year.

3. Mr. and Mrs. Watson were in the hotel at seven.
   They weren't there at ten.
   Mr. and Mrs. Watson were in the hotel at seven, but they weren't there at ten.

Join the two sentences. Use *but*. (negative sentence/affirmative sentence)

1. I wasn't here yesterday. I was here all day today.
   I wasn't here yesterday, but I was here all day today.

2. He isn't from China. He's Chinese.
   ....

3. She wasn't busy this morning. She was very busy this afternoon.
   ....

4. Mr. Black isn't here today. He was in yesterday.
   ....

5. They weren't sick last night. They were sick this morning.
   ....

2   Past of *BE:* Yes/No Questions and Short Answers

Take the part of Speaker A. Form yes/no questions.

	SPEAKER A	SPEAKER B
STATEMENT OF FACT	YES/NO QUESTION	AFFIRMATIVE SHORT ANSWER
1. THEY WERE SICK.	*Were they sick?*	Yes, they were.
2. MARY WAS LATE.	*Was Mary late?*	Yes, she was.
3. TOM WAS HERE YESTERDAY.	..............?	Yes, he was.
4. THE RADIO WAS A GIFT.	..............?	Yes, it was.
5. THEY WERE IN THE HOTEL.	..............?	Yes, they were.
6. FRED WAS BORN IN NEW YORK.	..............?	Yes, he was.
7. THAT WAS HIS SISTER.	..............?	Yes, it was.
8. HER FATHER WAS FROM MONTREAL.	..............?	Yes, he was.

Repeat after Speaker B.

SPEAKER A	SPEAKER B
YES/NO QUESTION	NEGATIVE SHORT ANSWER
1. Were you in the office yesterday?	No, I wasn't.
2. Was Jim born in New York?	No, he wasn't.
3. Were Tom and Ted absent today?	No, they weren't.
4. Was that your watch on the table?	No, it wasn't.
5. Was Mary busy?	No, she wasn't.
6. Were we very late?	No, we weren't.

Take the part of Speaker B. Give short answers as indicated.

SPEAKER A	SPEAKER B
YES/NO QUESTION	SHORT ANSWER
1. Were Dr. Black and his wife in the hotel?	No, ...
2. Were you born in Chicago?	No, ...
3. Was your sister here all day yesterday?	Yes, ...
4. Was that your son in the picture?	No, ...

5. Was Lesson 9 easy? Yes, ...
6. Was Mr. Ross an engineer? No, ...
7. Was that a business letter for me? No, ...
8. Were Ted and Helen married last week? Yes, ...
9. Were we here on Tuesday? No, ...
10. Was the watch a gift? Yes, ...

3 Cardinal Numbers: Twenty to One Hundred

Learn these numbers. First repeat them.

20	twenty	30	thirty	40	forty
21	twenty-one	31	thirty-one	50	fifty
22	twenty-two	32	thirty-two	60	sixty
23	twenty-three	33	thirty-three	70	seventy
	etc.		*etc.*	80	eighty
				90	ninety
				100	one hundred
					(or) a hundred

Practice reading these numbers.

21	22	23	24	25	26	27	28	29	30
71	72	73	74	75	76	77	78	79	80
1	11	21	31	41	51	61	71	81	91
4	14	24	34	44	54	64	74	84	94
6	39	64	71	97	55	41	19	77	82

4 Practice in Counting

Count by tens to 100.

10	20	30	40	50	60	70	80	90	100

Count by fives to 100.

5	10	15	20	25	30	35	40	45	50
55	60	65	70	75	80	85	90	95	100

Count by twos from 20 to 40.

20 22 24 26 28 30 32 34 36 38 40

5 Telling Age: *BE (10) years old*

Add a second sentence. Begin, *Last year* . . . .

1. I'm 32 years old.   *Last year I was 31.*
2. He's 46 years old.   . . . .
3. My sister's 29.   . . . .
4. My father's 66 years old.   . . . .
5. I'm 19 years old.   . . . .
6. Ellie's 10 years old.   . . . .

Add a second sentence. Begin, *Now* . . . . Use pronoun subjects.

1. Last year I was 23 years old.   *Now I'm 24.*
2. Last year she was 32 years old.   *Now she's 33.*
3. Last year my brother was 21 years old.   . . . .
4. Last year Tom was 16.   . . . .
5. Last year Jim was 19 years old.   . . . .
6. Last year my father was 54.   . . . .
7. Last year they were 76 years old.   . . . .

6 Questions with *did* and Short Answers with *did* and *didn't*

Repeat these questions.

Did your mother come?   Did you understand the dialog?
Did my brother call?   Did they speak English to you?
Did your sister stay there?   Did the Carlsons remember Tom Evers?

Take the part of Speaker B. Use the cue and give an affirmative or negative short answer.

SPEAKER A	SPEAKER B
1. Did your mother come? *(yes)*	*Yes, she did.*
2. Did your sister come, too? *(no)*	*No, she didn't.*

3. Did your brother and sister stay in New York? *(yes)*   <u>Yes, they did.</u>
4. Did you and Jim meet Jane? *(yes)*   <u>Yes, we did.</u>
5. Did Mr. and Mrs. Black believe you? *(no)*   ....
6. Did you repeat the dialog? *(yes)*   ....
7. Did Mary close the door? *(no)*   ....
8. Did your father work last Tuesday? *(no)*   ....
9. Did you say Eric was a scientist? *(yes)*   ....
10. Did Mr. and Mrs. Carlson come to dinner? *(yes)*   ....
11. Did you and Bill see John? *(no)*   ....
12. Did you study last night? *(yes)*   ....

PRONUNCIATION PRACTICE

1 Pronunciation of *13* and *30*, *14* and *40*, etc.

Repeat these pairs of numbers.

thirty	thirteen
forty	fourteen
fifty	fifteen
sixty	sixteen
seventy	seventeen
eighty	eighteen
ninety	nineteen

2 Number Discrimination

Listen. Say *one* if the speaker says the phrase in Column 1. Say *two* if he pronounces the phrase in Column 2.

(1)	(2)
forty boys	fourteen boys
eighty pages	eighteen pages
thirty children	thirteen children
fifty books	fifteen books
seventy men	seventeen men
ninety years	nineteen years
sixty schools	sixteen schools

NEW VOCABULARY IN LESSON 10

NOUNS	VERBS	ADJECTIVES	CARDINAL NUMBERS
city day hotel nationality night year	speak understand	absent easy	twenty-one, twenty-two, twenty-three, twenty-four, twenty-five, twenty-six, twenty-seven, twenty-eight, twenty-nine, thirty, forty, fifty, sixty, seventy, eighty, ninety, one hundred

GRAMMAR WORDS	EXPRESSIONS	NAMES

Noun Determiner: every
Contractions:
  wasn't weren't
Conjunction: but
	all day today
	every day
	I don't know.
		Family Names:
		  Clark Penny Yang
		  King Perez
		Place Names:
		  China New York Tokyo

LESSON 11

READING: RODNEY HILL WATSON

My name's Rod Watson. My full name is Rodney Hill Watson. I'm Bob Watson's brother, and I live in Denver, Colorado. Colorado is one of the western states of the United States.

I live in that house over there. I live on Clayton Street. The number is 1490. My address is 1490 Clayton Street. Both Bob and I were born in Denver, but Bob lives in Madison, Wisconsin now. I was born in 1937. My birthday is March 1. Bob was born in 1941.

I'm a government employee. I'm an economist. I work downtown in a large office building. I have a nice office there. I enjoy my work very much.

PRACTICE DRILLS AND EXERCISES

1   Giving Dates

Repeat these dates.

1419	(fourteen nineteen)	1601	(sixteen oh one)
1810	(eighteen ten)	1975	(nineteen seventy-five)
960	(nine sixty)	1942	(nineteen forty-two)

Take the part of Speaker B. Give short answers as in the models.

		SPEAKER A	SPEAKER B
	STATEMENT OF FACT	WH- QUESTION	SHORT ANSWER
1.	ROD WAS BORN IN 1937.	When was Rod born?	In 1937.
2.	KATHY WAS BORN IN 1964.	When was Kathy born?	In 1964.
3.	JIM WAS BORN IN 1955.	When was Jim born?	....
4.	MR. CHANG WAS BORN IN 1915.	When was Mr. Chang born?	....
5.	MRS. LOO WAS BORN IN 1926.	When was Mrs. Loo born?	....
6.	BETTY WAS BORN IN 1949.	When was Betty born?	....
7.	TOM WAS BORN IN 1972.	When was Tom born?	....
8.	MR. HIGH WAS BORN IN 1889.	When was Mr. High born?	....

2 Giving Street Addresses

Repeat these addresses.

STREET	AVENUE/ROAD/LANE
14 Long Street	1216 Western Avenue
2119 Fall Street	4229 Flower Avenue
6239 Jefferson Street	960 River Road
3013 Main Street	1236 Branch Road
1490 Clayton Street	5916 Rose Lane
4441 First Street	1900 Oak Lane

Substitute the addresses.

What's your address?

I live at *1419 Long Street.*
I live at *1630 Main Avenue.* (1630 Main Avenue)
.... (121 Jefferson Street)
.... (6262 Rose Lane)
.... (1880 River Road)
.... (1205 Western Avenue)

3   Conjunction (with Deletion): *and ... too*

Repeat the sentences.

1. He's Spanish.
   She's Spanish, too.
      He's Spanish and she is, too.

2. They were early yesterday.
   We were early yesterday, too.
      They were early yesterday, and we were, too.

3. He was born in 1953.
   She was born in 1953, too.
      He was born in 1953, and she was, too.

4. My office is at 44 Main Street.
   Her office is at 44 Main Street, too.
      My office is at 44 Main Street, and her office is, too.

5. John was quite late this morning.
   We were quite late, too.
      John was quite late this morning, and we were, too.

4   Questions with *do* and *does*

Repeat these questions.

Do you enjoy your work?	Does she live in Japan?
Do we know her?	Does he work downtown?
Do they speak English?	Does Tom speak Spanish?

Take the part of Speaker B. Answer the questions.

	SPEAKER A	SPEAKER B
1.	Where does Rod Watson live?	*He lives in Denver.*
2.	Does he live on Madison Street?	*No. He lives on Clayton Street.*
3.	What does Rod Watson do?	*He works for the government.*
4.	What do you do?	....

UNIT 3 LESSON 11 | 81

5. Where do you work? ....
6. Do you live in Denver? ....
7. Where do you live? ....
8. When do you study? ....
9. Where do you study? ....

5 Past of *BE*: Negative Questions

Take the part of Speaker B. Form a negative question. Use subject pronouns.

1. SPEAKER A Bob Watson was born in 1941. *(in 1937)*
   SPEAKER B *Oh, wasn't he born in 1937?*
   SPEAKER A No, his brother was born then.

2. SPEAKER A Jane Carlson was born in Montreal. *(in Minnesota)*
   SPEAKER B *Oh, wasn't she born in Minnesota?*
   SPEAKER A No, her husband was born there.

3. SPEAKER A The pencils were green. *(red)*
   SPEAKER B ....?
   SPEAKER A No, the pens were red.

4. SPEAKER A Miss Long was late today. *(on time)*
   SPEAKER B ....?
   SPEAKER A No, but she was on time yesterday.

5. SPEAKER A The Nelsons were married in 1962. *(in 1960)*
   SPEAKER B ....?
   SPEAKER A No, the Taylors were married then.

6. SPEAKER A Mr. Brown was out. *(in)*
   SPEAKER B ....?
   SPEAKER A No, but his secretary was in.

THE ALPHABET

This is the English alphabet. First listen to the speaker say the alphabet and then repeat the letters.

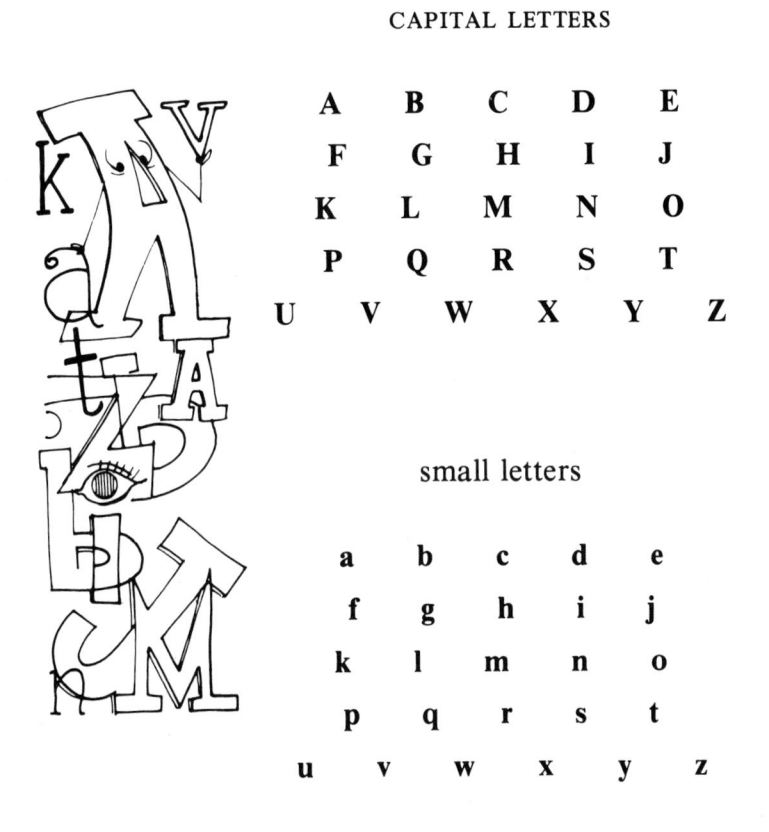

CAPITAL LETTERS

A B C D E
F G H I J
K L M N O
P Q R S T
U V W X Y Z

small letters

a b c d e
f g h i j
k l m n o
p q r s t
u v w x y z

Repeat the sentences.

1. My name's Watson. That's W-a-t-s-o-n.
2. My first name's Rodney, R-o-d-n-e-y.
3. You spell *address,* a-d-d-r-e-s-s.
4. *Quite* is spelled q-u-i-t-e.

Listen.

SPEAKER A	SPEAKER B
How do you spell *husband*?	h-u-s-b-a-n-d
How do you spell *friend*?	f-r-i-e-n-d
Do you spell *Rebecca* with two c's?	That's right. It's R-e-b-e-c-c-a.
Can you spell *radio*?	Yes, that's easy. It's r-a-d-i-o.

Write the words as they are spelled by the teacher. (Use a separate piece of paper.)

	TEACHER	STUDENT
Examples:	n-i-c-e	*nice*
	l-a-r-g-e	*large*

NEW VOCABULARY IN LESSON 11

NOUNS		VERBS	ADVERB	ADJECTIVE
address	house	enjoy	downtown	western
avenue	lane	spell		
building	road			
economist	street			
employee				

GRAMMAR WORDS	NAMES
Question Word: when	Family Names:
Noun Determiner:	High Hill Loo
both	Masculine Names:
	Rodney/Rod
COMPOUND	Feminine Name: Rebecca
	Streets:
office building	Branch Flower River
	Clayton Jefferson Rose
EXPRESSIONS	Fall Main Western
	First Oak
Can you spell...?	
How do you spell...?	

Additional Words for Spelling Practice

l-a-n-e	m-a-r-r-i-e-d	d-o-o-r
c-i-t-y	p-i-c-t-u-r-e	s-t-r-e-e-t
h-o-t-e-l	s-e-v-e-n	c-l-o-c-k
b-o-r-n	w-a-t-c-h	v-e-r-y
o-f-f-i-c-e	l-e-t-t-e-r	b-u-s-y

LESSON 12

BASIC SENTENCES

Listen to these sentences. Then repeat them.

1. There are twelve months in a year.
2. They are January, February, March;
   April, May, June;
   July, August, September;
   October, November and December.
3. January is the first month.
4. February is the second month.
5. March is the third month.
6. This is the fourth of January.
7. This is January 4. *(January the fourth* or *January fourth)*
8. This is the fifth of February.
9. This is February 5. *(February the fifth* or *February fifth)*
10. This is the sixth of April.
11. This is April 6. *(April the sixth* or *April sixth)*
12. Today is the seventh of July.
13. Tomorrow is the eighth of July.
14. Now it's September.
15. September is the ninth month.
16. Next month is October.
17. It's the tenth month.
18. November is the eleventh month.
19. December is the twelfth month of the year.
20. January is the first month and December is the twelfth month.

PRACTICE DRILLS AND EXERCISES (1)

1 Ordinal Numbers

Repeat the ordinal numbers.

CARDINAL	ORDINAL		CARDINAL	ORDINAL	
1	1st	first	20	20th	twentieth
2	2nd	second	21	21st	twenty-first
3	3rd	third	22	22nd	twenty-second
4	4th	fourth	23	23rd	twenty-third
5	5th	fifth			
6	6th	sixth	30	30th	thirtieth
7	7th	seventh	31	31st	thirty-first
8	8th	eighth	32	32nd	thirty-second
9	9th	ninth	33	33rd	thirty-third
10	10th	tenth			
11	11th	eleventh	40	40th	fortieth
12	12th	twelfth	50	50th	fiftieth
13	13th	thirteenth	60	60th	sixtieth
14	14th	fourteenth	70	70th	seventieth
15	15th	fifteenth	80	80th	eightieth
16	16th	sixteenth	90	90th	ninetieth
17	17th	seventeenth	100	100th	hundredth (or one hundredth)
18	18th	eighteenth			
19	19th	nineteenth			

2 Dates

Read these dates.

1. April 18 (April eighteenth)
2. March 3
3. June 21
4. August 30
5. October 10
6. February 19
7. May 26
8. July 4

Now read these dates.

1. March 16, 1926
2. October 4, 1957
3. April 12, 1961
4. March 18, 1965
5. July 20, 1969
6. December 11, 1972

CONVERSATION PRACTICE

Listen to this conversation. Then repeat.

Bob asks questions; Fred answers.

1. What's the date today?
    It's the fourteenth of June.
2. Isn't today the thirteenth?
    No. Today's the fourteenth.
    Yesterday was the thirteenth.
3. Wasn't your birthday on the tenth?
    No. My birthday's the eleventh.
    My brother was born on the tenth.
4. What year were you born in?
    1955.
    I was 21 last week.
5. Weren't you born in Chicago?
    Well, not exactly.
    I was born in a little town near Chicago.

			JUNE			
S	M	T	W	T	F	S
			1	2	3	4	5
6	7	8	9	10	11	12
13	(14)	15	16	17	18	19
20	21	22	23	24	25	26
27	28	29	30			

PRACTICE DRILLS AND EXERCISES (2)

1 Negative Questions with BE: Past Tense

Speaker A: Fill the blanks with *wasn't* or *weren't*.
Speaker B: Reply with short answers.

SPEAKER A	SPEAKER B
1. *Wasn't* yesterday your birthday?	No, *it wasn't*.
2. .... you late?	....
3. .... Mr. and Mrs. Black in the hotel?	....
4. .... Mr. Smith in?	....

5. .... we on time? ....
6. .... Tom and Becky married last year? ....
7. .... Bob White born in Denver? ....
8. .... Mrs. Carlson born in Toronto? ....

2 BE: Past Tense

Fill the blanks with the correct form of *was/were* or *wasn't/weren't*.

1. I'm here today, but I *wasn't* here yesterday.
2. I'm not early today, but I .... early yesterday.
3. We're here now, but we .... here yesterday.
4. Kim wasn't born in Korea. She .... born in Burma.
5. This isn't January. Last month .... January.
6. My mother wasn't tall, but my father .... very tall.
7. We're married now, but we .... married last year.
8. Mrs. Black was in the hotel, but Mr. Black .... there.
9. She wasn't born in Denver, but her sister .... born there.
10. I wasn't busy in January, but I .... very busy in February.

3 Reading Dates

DATES ARE OFTEN WRITTEN IN NUMBERS.

Listen.

MONTH DAY
5/10 (May tenth)
7/8 (July eighth)
2/4 (February fourth)

MONTH DAY YEAR
5/10/72 (May 10, 1972)
12/31/49 (December 31, 1949)
4-1-61 (April 1, 1961)

Read these dates.

(a) 10/10   (d) 1/1/80   (g) 2/14/40
(b) 7/8   (e) 3-5-69   (h) 9-1-25
(c) 6/4   (f) 5/14/73   (i) 1/13/55

4 Polite Expressions

Repeat these expressions and learn them.

It's so good to see you!

I'm so glad you could come.

Please come in.

Come in and sit down.

Let me take your coat.

Please make yourself at home.

LISTENING PRACTICE: DINNER PARTY AT THE WATSONS'

The Watsons invited the Carlsons and the Lings for dinner. As the dialog opens, Mr. and Mrs. Carlson come to the door.

(the doorbell rings)

MRS. WATSON   Bob, the Carlsons are here.

MR. WATSON   Okay, I'm coming.

MRS. WATSON   Oh, hello.
I'm so glad you could come.
Please come in.

MRS. CARLSON   Hello.
Barbara, I want you to meet my husband, Eric.

MRS. WATSON   How do you do?

MR. CARLSON   So nice to meet you, Mrs. Watson.

MRS. WATSON   And this is my husband, Bob.

MR. WATSON   How do you do?
Please come in.
Let me take your coats.

MRS. WATSON   Come in, please.
Please sit down.

MR. WATSON   Where are you from, Mr. Carlson?

MR. CARLSON   My family's from Sweden.
But I was born in Minnesota.
Jane's Canadian.

MRS. WATSON   Yes, we know.
She was born in Montreal.

MR. WATSON   I understand you're a chemist, Mr. Carlson.

MR. CARLSON   Yes, I'm with the Lamar Lumber Company.

(the doorbell rings)

MRS. WATSON   Excuse me.
Fred and Irene Ling are here.

NEW VOCABULARY IN LESSON 12

NOUNS		VERBS	ADJECTIVE	ADVERBS
coat	month	let	next (+ month)	exactly
date	party	make		tomorrow
father	town	take		
		understand		

GRAMMAR WORDS

Preposition: near
Intensifier: so

EXPRESSIONS

I'm (so) glad you could come.
Let me take your coat.
Make yourself at home.
There are . . . .

COMPOUND

dinner party

ORDINAL NUMBERS

first, second, third, fourth, fifth, sixth, seventh, eighth, ninth, tenth, eleventh, twelfth, thirteenth, fourteenth, fifteenth, sixteenth, seventeenth, eighteenth, nineteenth, twentieth, thirtieth, fortieth, fiftieth, sixtieth, seventieth, eightieth, ninetieth, one hundredth, twenty-first, twenty-second, twenty-third, etc.

MONTHS

January, February, March, April, May, June, July, August, September, October, November, December

NAMES:

Place Names: Burma   Toronto
Feminine Name: Kim

UNIT 4

THE PEOPLE IN UNIT 4

KATHLEEN (KATHY) JOHNSON
(friend of Ellie Watson)
Age 10
Neighbor and schoolmate
of Ellie Watson

ALICE HAYES
(friend of Jim Carter)
Age 18
Senior in high school
Jim Carter's favorite
girl friend

LESSON 13

DIALOGS

Dialog 1: Jim Carter

Jim has been fishing all day. He returns to the Watson home (he is staying there for the summer) and finds Mr. Watson in the living room. They talk.

JIM	Hi.
MR. WATSON	Hi, Jim. Come on in and sit down. Are you going to the movies with us tonight?
JIM	What time are you going?
MR. WATSON	About nine o'clock.
JIM	No, I guess not. I'm pretty tired.
MR. WATSON	What were you doing all day?
JIM	I was fishing on the lake.
MR. WATSON	Any luck?
JIM	No. Two small ones.

Dialog 2: Mrs. Watson Comes Home

Mrs. Watson comes home from a shopping trip. She has an armful of packages and she looks tired. She lets herself in the door and calls out.

MRS. WATSON	Hello. Anybody home?
MR. WATSON	Hi. We're in the living room.
MRS. WATSON	Where are the children?
MR. WATSON	They're in their rooms. Ellie's studying. And I think Tom's looking at TV.

JIM Let me take your packages.
MRS. WATSON Oh, thanks, Jim.
MR. WATSON I have a good idea.
We're all going out to dinner tonight.
MRS. WATSON Oh, good. I'm tired.
Jim, are you coming with us?
JIM Of course. I'm hungry!

BASIC SENTENCES (1)

Listen to these sentences. Then repeat them.

1. It's one o'clock. (1:00)
2. It's two o'clock. (2:00) 
3. It's three a.m. (3:00 a.m.) 
4. It's three o'clock in the morning. (3:00 a.m.)
5. It's four p.m. (4:00 p.m.) 
6. It's exactly four. (4:00)
7. It's five o'clock sharp. (5:00) 
8. I come at one-thirty p.m. (1:30 p.m.) 
9. I come at half past one. (1:30)

UNIT 4 LESSON 13 | 95

10. I leave at six-thirty p.m. (6:30 p.m.)
11. I leave at half past six. (6:30)

12. It's 7:10.
13. It's seven ten.
14. It's exactly ten past seven.
15. It's 7:10 in the evening.
    It's 7:10 p.m.

16. Now it's seven eighteen. (7:18)
17. It's eighteen after seven. (7:18)

18. The train leaves at nine-oh-two. (9:02)
19. It leaves at two minutes after nine. (9:02)

20. She's coming at seven fifteen. (7:15)
21. She's coming at a quarter past seven. (7:15)
22. She's coming at a quarter after seven. (7:15)

PRACTICE DRILLS AND EXERCISES (1)
1 Telling Time
Give the time in numbers.

1. It's ten minutes after nine.

    It's 9:10. (nine ten) . . . .

2. It's twenty minutes past three.

    . . . .

3. It's a quarter past eight.

   . . . .

4. It's half past nine.

   . . . .

5. It's nineteen minutes past ten.

   . . . .

6. It's half past eleven.

   . . . .

7. It's four minutes past two.

   . . . .

8. It's six minutes after five.

   . . . .

2 Telling Time

Repeat.

What time is it?

It's exactly *nine minutes after nine.*

It's exactly *three o'clock.*

It's exactly *a quarter after one.*

It's exactly *four oh one.*

It's exactly *half past eleven.*

3 The *-ing* Form of Verbs

Repeat these verbs and their *-ing* forms.

go	going	ride	riding
study	studying	have	having
walk	walking	type	typing
talk	talking	come	coming
look	looking	practice	practicing
fish	fishing	shop	shopping

Fill in the -ing forms of the verbs and repeat both forms.

enjoy	....	leave	....
call	....	make	....
do	....	hope	....
help	....	take	....
feel	....	live	....
work	....	sit	....

4   Present Continuous: Action Occurring at the Moment of Speech (New Vocabulary)

Repeat these sentences.

(a) He's walking.

(b) He's fishing.

(c) She's typing a letter.

(d) We're listening to the radio.

(e) They're watching TV.

(f) He's reading the newspaper.

98 | UNIT 4 LESSON 13

(g) She's riding a bicycle.

(h) They're studying.

(i) She's shopping for groceries.

(j) We're buying clothes.

BASIC SENTENCES (2)

Listen to these sentences. Then repeat them.

1. It's seven thirty-five. (7:35)

2. Now it's seven forty. (7:40)

3. John's coming at seven forty-five. (7:45)

4. We're leaving at seven fifty. (7:50)

5. We'll be there at seven fifty-eight. (7:58)

6. It's twenty-five minutes to nine.

7. Now it's twenty before nine.

8. Mary's coming at a quarter to nine.

9. Nancy and Mary are leaving at ten to nine.

10. They'll be there at two minutes to eight.

11. It's 7:30 a.m.
12. It's seven thirty in the morning.
13. It's 7:30 p.m.
14. It's seven thirty in the evening.

15. It's 10:30 p.m.
16. It's 10:30 at night.

17. It's noon.
18. It's twelve o'clock.

19. It's midnight.
20. It's twelve o'clock.
21. It's twelve o'clock midnight.

PRACTICE DRILLS AND EXERCISES (2)

1 Telling Time

Give the time in numbers.

1. It's a quarter to three.

    It's 2:45. . . . .

2. It's a quarter to nine.

    . . . .

3. It's a quarter to one.

    . . . .

4. It's a quarter to five.

    . . . .

UNIT 4 LESSON 13 | 101

5. It's a quarter to twelve.
   ....

6. It's a quarter to six.
   ....

Give the time in numbers.

1. It's eight minutes to eight.
   It's 7:52. ....

2. It's twenty minutes to six.
   ....

3. It's five to four.
   ....

4. It's a quarter to six.
   ....

5. It's twenty-five to eleven.
   ....

6. It's eighteen before five.
   ....

7. It's a quarter to two.
   ....

8. It's twenty-one minutes to nine.
   ....

2 Asking about Time

Repeat these questions and answers about time.

SPEAKER A	SPEAKER B
Is it *five* o'clock yet?	Yes, it's a few minutes after *five*.
Is it *six* o'clock yet?	Yes, it's a few minutes after *six*.
Is it *nine* o'clock yet?	Yes, it's a few minutes after *nine*.
Is it *eleven* o'clock yet?	Yes, it's a few minutes after *eleven*.

Is it *five* o'clock yet?
Is it *two* o'clock yet?
Is it *ten* o'clock yet?
Is it *six* o'clock yet?

Is it exactly *four* o'clock?
Is it exactly *two fifteen*?
Is it exactly *nine* o'clock?
Is it exactly *six thirty*?

What time is it?

No, but it's almost *five*.
No, but it's almost *two*.
No, but it's almost *ten*.
No, but it's almost *six*.

Yes, it's *four o'clock* sharp.
Yes, it's *two fifteen* sharp.
Yes, it's *nine o'clock* sharp.
Yes, it's *six thirty* sharp.

Let's see. It's just *four o'clock*.
Let's see. It's just *nine eighteen*.
Let's see. It's just *noon*.
Let's see. It's just *midnight*.
Let's see. It's just *three fifty*.

NEW VOCABULARY IN LESSON 13

NOUNS		VERBS	ADJECTIVES	ADVERBS
bicycle	movie	buy	hungry	about
clothes	noon	fish	tired	almost
evening	package	guess		a.m.
groceries	quarter	leave		p.m.
half	time	practice		tonight
idea	TV	read		yet
lake		ride		
luck		shop		
		walk		
		watch		
		type		

GRAMMAR WORDS

Noun Determiner: any
Possessive Determiner:
  their
Object Pronouns:
  me   us
Noun Substitutes:
  anybody ones
Contraction: they'll
Prepositions:
  after   past
Intensifier: pretty

EXPRESSIONS

a few minutes
at night
be tired
Come on.
half past (one)
I guess not.
Let's see.
(one) o'clock
  sharp
of course

COMPOUNDS

living room
midnight
newspaper

NAMES

Family Name:
  Hayes
Feminine Names:
  Alice
  Nancy

LESSON 14

DIALOG FOR COMPREHENSION: TELEPHONE CONVERSATION

Listen to this dialog several times. Make sure you understand it. Learn the new words.

(telephone rings)

KATHY	Hello.
ELLIE	Hello. Kathy?
KATHY	Yes. Who's this?
ELLIE	This is Ellie. What are you doing?
KATHY	I'm studying.
ELLIE	English or history?
KATHY	History.
ELLIE	I'm studying history, too. This is a hard lesson.
KATHY	Are you answering the questions on page 19?
ELLIE	Yes, I'm doing them now. I am having trouble with question six.
KATHY	Let's see. Oh, yes. I'm having trouble with that, too.

(Mother calls)

ELLIE	Oh, Mom's calling. Dinner's ready. Call me later, will you? Good-bye.
KATHY	O.K. . . . 'Bye.

PRACTICE DRILLS AND EXERCISES (1)

1 Present Continuous: Affirmative

Repeat the first sentence. Then substitute the subject noun or pronoun.

1. *I'm* studying English.
2. *He's* studying English. *(He's)*
3. .... *(We're)*
4. .... *(They're)*
5. .... *(Mrs. Watson's)*
6. .... *(My friend's)*

Repeat the first sentence. Then make new sentences.

1. *Kathy's* having trouble with history.
2. *I'm* having trouble with history. *(I'm)*
3. .... *(Her friend's)*
4. .... *(Jack's)*
5. .... *(They're)*
6. .... *(Jack and Kathy)*

2 Present Continuous: Yes/No Questions and Short Answers

Repeat the yes/no questions after Speaker A.

	STATEMENT OF FACT (AFFIRMATIVE)	SPEAKER A YES/NO QUESTION	SPEAKER B SHORT ANSWER
1.	ELLIE'S STUDYING.	Is Ellie studying?	Yes, she is.
2.	TOM'S WATCHING TV.	Is Tom watching TV?	Yes, he is.
3.	THEY'RE SITTING DOWN.	Are they sitting down?	Yes, they are.

Study this section and then listen to the questions and answers.

(Note: Using the negative statement of fact, Speaker A forms a simple yes/no question (not a negative question) to ask of Speaker B. Speaker B then gives a short negative answer to correspond with the negative statement of fact.)

STATEMENT OF FACT (NEGATIVE)	SPEAKER A YES/NO QUESTION	SPEAKER B SHORT ANSWER
1. KATHY ISN'T STUDYING.	Is Kathy studying?	No, she isn't.
2. BILL ISN'T WATCHING TV.	Is Bill watching TV?	No, he isn't.
3. THEY AREN'T STANDING UP.	Are they standing up?	No, they aren't.

Take the part of Speaker A. Form simple yes/no questions.

STATEMENT OF FACT	SPEAKER A YES/NO QUESTION	SPEAKER B SHORT ANSWER
1. HELEN'S SHOPPING.	*Is Helen shopping?*	Yes, she is.
2. THEY AREN'T RIDING BICYCLES.	*Are they riding bicycles?*	No, they aren't.
3. KATHY'S LOOKING AT TV.	. . . . ?	Yes, ...
4. THEY AREN'T LIVING HERE NOW.	. . . . ?	No, ...
5. FRED'S WALKING TO WORK.	. . . . ?	Yes, ...
6. THEY AREN'T GOING NOW.	. . . . ?	No, ...
7. MISS WILSON'S TYPING.	. . . . ?	Yes, ...
8. MISS GREEN ISN'T TYPING NOW.	. . . . ?	No, ...

3 Present Continuous: Negative Forms

Listen to the model. Then say the sentences.

a.

He isn't reading a book.
He's reading a newspaper.

b.

They aren't buying clothes.
They're shopping for groceries.

c.

Ellie isn't watching TV.
She's studying.

d.

We aren't sleeping.
We're fishing.

4 Present Tense *(every day)* and Present Continuous *(now/right now):* Contrast

Repeat the third sentence in each group.

We practice every day.
We're not practicing now.
    We practice every day, but we're not practicing now.

They fish every day.
They're not fishing right now.
    They fish every day, but they're not fishing right now.

The children study every day.
They're not studying now.
    The children study every day, but they're not studying now.

I work hard every day.
I'm not working hard right now.
    I work hard every day, but I'm not working hard right now.

5 Present Continuous: with Various Time Expressions*

Listen. Then repeat.

a. *this week*

    at home

    at home this week

    working at home this week

  Mr. Carlson's working at home this week.

b. *this month*

    at the hospital

    at the hospital this month

    working at the hospital this month

  Mrs. Watson's working at the hospital this month.

---

*Notice that the action expressed by the present continuous does not necessarily go on at the time of speech.

c. *this year*

at the university

at the university this year

studying at the university this year

Jim's studying at the university this year.

QUESTIONS AND ANSWERS

Listen to these questions and answers. Then repeat.

1. Were you busy yesterday?
    Yes. I was.
    I was writing a report.
2. Was Jim home yesterday?
    No, he wasn't.
    He was fishing all day.
3. Isn't this your pen, Chuck?
    Yes, it is.
    Thank you.
    I was looking for it.
4. What was Ellie doing?
    She was talking to Kathy on the phone.
    They were talking about their history lesson.
5. Why are you so late, Kathy?
    I was helping the teacher, Mom.
6. Isn't Mrs. Watson home?
    No, she isn't.
    She's working at the hospital this week.
7. Were Jack and Kathy at the party?
    Yes, they were.
    Twelve boys and nine girls were there.
8. Were they playing games?
    Oh, my, yes.
    They were singing and dancing and having a good time!

PRACTICE DRILLS AND EXERCISES (2)

1 Past Continuous: Two Subjects and Two Actions*

Combine these sentences with *and*.

They were singing.
We were dancing.
They were singing and we were dancing. . . . .

Ellie was watching TV.
Tom was sleeping.
Ellie was watching TV and Tom was sleeping. . . . .

Jim was fishing all afternoon.
Mr. Watson was writing a report.
. . . .

I was studying.
The children were talking.
. . . .

2 Present and Past Continuous: Short Answers

Fill in the blanks and repeat.

SPEAKER A	SPEAKER B
	(Give short answers)
. . . . . . you living here now?	Yes, ...
. . . . . . she taking a walk?	Yes, ...
. . . . . . Jim working?	No, ...
. . . . . . Mary studying history last night?	No, ...
. . . . . . they feeling well?	Yes, ...
. . . . . . Mr. and Mrs. Watson working in New York?	No, ...
. . . . . . Ellie studying history right now?	Yes, ...

*The actions in these sentences are taking place concurrently, or at the same time.

..... you and Mrs. Black living in Chicago last year?   No, ...

..... Mrs. Watson calling Ellie?   Yes, ...

..... Jim writing a report last night?   No, ...

..... the students sleeping in class?   No, ...

READING: ELLIE VISITS HER GRANDPARENTS

I wasn't in school yesterday. I was absent. I was visiting my grandparents. They have a beautiful farm in the country. The farmhouse is beautiful, too. It's not very big, but it's very nice. My mother was born there. My grandfather was born there, too.

    My grandparents are getting old now, but they're still working. My grandfather's about sixty. He's still farming. My grandmother's still taking care of the house. She's a very good cook. I always have a good time there. I always like to see my grandparents and I like to eat, too—especially Grandmother's cookies.

NEW VOCABULARY IN LESSON 14

NOUNS	VERBS	ADJECTIVES	ADVERBS

cook   grandparent
cookie   history
country   Mom
  (rural)   phone
farm   report
game   trouble
grandfather
grandmother
	cook
	dance
	eat
	farm
	play
	sing
	visit
		beautiful
		hard
		  (difficult)
		ready
			always
			especially
			later
			still

GRAMMAR WORDS	EXPRESSIONS	COMPOUNDS

Object Pronouns:
  it   them
	'Bye
	Good-bye.
	have a good time
	have trouble with
	look for
	take care of
	. . . will you?
		farmhouse
		history lesson
		telephone conversation
		
		NAME
		Masculine Name:
		  Chuck

LESSON 15
DIALOG: WHAT DAY IS IT?

PHIL   What day is it?

LUIS   It's Monday.

PHIL   Are you sure it isn't Tuesday?

LUIS   Yes, I'm sure.
It's Monday.
It's Monday, January 12.
I'm looking at today's newspaper.

PHIL   So, it's the first day of a new week!

LUIS   First day?
It's the second day.
Sunday's the first day of the week.

It's Sunday, Monday, Tuesday, Wednesday, Thursday, Friday, Saturday.

PHIL   Are you crazy?
Monday's the first day.
Sunday's on the *weekend*.

LUIS   No, no. You're all wrong.
Get a calendar and I'll show you.

PHIL   Well, here's the calendar.
See.... It's Sun...

LUIS   ...day, Monday, Tuesday, Wednesday, Thursday, Friday, Saturday.

PRACTICE DRILLS AND EXERCISES (1)

1   Days of the Week and Replacement of Place Adverbial with *there*

Repeat.

SPEAKER A	SPEAKER B
When were you in *New York?*	I was there last *Tuesday.*
When were you in *London?*	I was there last *Monday.*
When were you in *Tokyo?*	I was there last *Friday.*
When were you in *Bangkok?*	I was there last *Wednesday.*
When were you in *Lisbon?*	I was there last *Thursday.*

2   Practice with Days of the Week

Take the part of Speaker B.

A   Isn't today Monday?

B   *No, it's Tuesday.*

A   Isn't today Friday?

B   ....

A   Isn't today Saturday?

B   ....

UNIT 4 LESSON 15 | 115

A   Isn't today Wednesday?

B   . . . .

A   Isn't today Thursday?

B   . . . .

A   Isn't today Tuesday?

B   . . . .

3   Practice with Days of the Week

Form a third sentence.

Yesterday wasn't Sunday.
Yesterday was Monday.
   Yesterday wasn't Sunday; it was Monday.

Tomorrow's not Monday.
Tomorrow's Tuesday.
   Tomorrow's not Monday; it's Tuesday.

Today isn't Friday.
Today's Thursday.
   . . . .

Today's not Wednesday.
Today's Friday.
   . . . .

This isn't Friday night.
This is Saturday night.
   . . . .

Tomorrow's not Sunday.
Tomorrow's Saturday.

....

4 **Future: Present Continuous + Future Time Expression**

Substitute the *future time expressions.*

He's leaving for London *tomorrow.*

He's leaving for London *on Thursday.* *(on Thursday)*

.... *(the day after tomorrow)*

.... *(next week)*

.... *(in an hour)*

.... *(Tuesday of next week)*

5 **Present Continuous: Question-word (Wh-) Questions with *When***

Complete the sentences.

STATEMENT OF FACT	SPEAKER A WH- QUESTION	SPEAKER B SHORT ANSWER
1. HE'S LEAVING IN A FEW MINUTES.	When's he leaving?	In a few minutes.
2. SHE'S COMING TOMORROW.	When's she coming?	Tomorrow.
3. THE PLANE'S ARRIVING AT NOON.	....	At noon.
4. THEY'RE HAVING DINNER AT SIX.	....	At six.
5.	When's she meeting John?	In an hour.
6.	When's he going back to Chicago?	Monday.
7. WE'RE LEAVING AT MIDNIGHT.	When are we leaving?	....
8. WE'RE EATING LUNCH AT 1:30.	When are we eating lunch?	....

UNIT 4 LESSON 15 | 117

6 Future Time with *will* (*I'll* and *We'll*)

Substitute progressively.

I'll see you tomorrow.

I'll see you *Thursday*.

We'll see you Thursday.

We'll *call you* Thursday.

We'll call you *in a few minutes*.

I'll call you in a few minutes.

.... *(in an hour)*

.... *(meet you)*

.... *(We'll)*

.... *(be there)*

.... *(at six sharp)*

.... *(I'll)*

.... *(We)*

.... *(call)*

.... *(in an hour)*

.... *(I)*

.... *(later)*

I'll see you later. .... *(see you)*

Questions and Answers

Listen to these questions and answers. Repeat the questions. Then repeat the answers.

1. What were you doing last night?
    Studying.
2. What were you studying?
    French and math.
3. When's Phil coming back home?
    On Tuesday.

4. When's Luis coming?
   Thursday.

5. Where are they living now?
   In New York.

6. What's Miss Green doing?
   Typing.

7. What's she typing?
   A letter for Mr. Jones.

8. What are you doing?
   Reading.

9. What are you reading?
   The morning paper.

10. What's Jim doing?
    Eating again.

11. What's he eating now?
    A sandwich.

PRACTICE DRILLS AND EXERCISES (2)

1   Short Answers to Question-word (Wh-) Questions

Study these examples.

1. When are you coming?

   At six o'clock.   (SHORT ANSWER)
   I'm coming at six o'clock.   (COMPLETE ANSWER)

2. When are you leaving for Singapore?

   Next Monday.   (SHORT ANSWER)
   I'm leaving for Singapore next Monday.   (COMPLETE ANSWER)

3. When's Mr. Smith arriving?

   On Tuesday.   (SHORT ANSWER)
   He's arriving on Tuesday.   (COMPLETE ANSWER)

Take the part of Speaker B. Give short answers.

STATEMENT OF FACT	SPEAKER A WH- QUESTION	SPEAKER B SHORT ANSWER
1. PHIL'S COMING AT NINE.	When's Phil coming?	*At nine.*
2. THE TRAIN'S ARRIVING AT 4:10.	When's the train arriving?	....
3. SHE'S GOING TO MADRID NEXT WEEK.	When's she going to Madrid?	....
4. WE'RE HAVING LUNCH AT ONE.	When are we having lunch?	....
5. SHE'S GOING TO PARIS TONIGHT.	When's she going to Paris?	....
6. THEY'RE HAVING THE MEETING AT FOUR.	When are they having the meeting?	....
7. HE'S GOING TO THE MOVIES AT EIGHT.	When's he going to the movies?	....

2 Present and Past Continuous: Question-word (Wh-) Questions and Short Answers

Study the questions and short answers. Repeat after Speaker A.

A   What was Ellie doing?
B   Studying.
A   What was she studying?
B   History.

ELLIE WAS STUDYING HISTORY.

A   What are the children doing?
B   Singing.
A   What are they singing?
B   "Happy Birthday."

THE CHILDREN ARE SINGING "HAPPY BIRTHDAY."

A What are they doing?
B Eating.
A What are they eating?
B Sandwiches.

THEY'RE EATING SANDWICHES.

A What's he doing?
B Reading.
A What's he reading?
B The paper.

HE'S READING THE PAPER.

Take the part of Speaker B. Give short answers.

A What's Betty doing?
B ....
A What's she studying?
B ....

BETTY'S STUDYING SPANISH.

A What's he doing?
B ....
A What's he writing?
B ....

HE'S WRITING A BOOK.

A What's she doing?
B ....
A What's she typing?
B ....

SHE'S TYPING A BUSINESS LETTER.

A What was Mrs. Carter doing?
B ....
A What was she cooking?
B ....

MRS. CARTER WAS COOKING FISH.

UNIT 4 LESSON 15 | 121

3 Present Continuous

Speaker A: Read the statement.
Speaker B: Form a question-word question.
Speaker A: Answer according to the picture.

A He isn't watching TV.
B *What is he doing?*
A *He's sleeping.*

A He isn't reading.
B *What is he doing?*
A *He's writing a report.*

A She isn't studying history.
B ....?
A ....

A They aren't working.
B ....?
A ....

A He isn't writing letters.

B ....?

A ....

A They aren't singing.

B ....?

A ....

A She isn't talking.

B ....?

A ....

DIALOG FOR COMPREHENSION: THE BIRTHDAY PARTY

Listen to the dialog several times. Make sure you understand it. Learn the new words.

UNIT 4 LESSON 15 | 123

Jim Carter (who is spending the summer at the home of his older sister, Mrs. Watson) has met a girl he likes very much—Alice Hayes. They are taking a walk together and are talking as they pass by the Watsons' house.

ALICE Who's singing in your house, Jim?

JIM It's Ellie and her friends.

ALICE Who's Ellie?

JIM She's my little niece.
It's her birthday.
They're singing "Happy Birthday."

ALICE Oh, I see.
How old is she?

JIM She's ten.

ALICE I suppose they're playing games?

JIM Oh, yes. Ellie was planning games all day yesterday.
By the way, Alice, when's your birthday?

ALICE Today.

JIM Today!

ALICE Yes.

JIM Well, imagine that! How old are you?

ALICE Eighteen.
By the way, some friends are having a party for me tonight.
Do you want to come?

JIM Very much. What time?

ALICE About 8:00.

JIM I'll be at your house about 7:30. Is that all right?

ALICE Fine.

JIM And, Alice...

ALICE Yes?

JIM Happy Birthday!

NEW VOCABULARY IN LESSON 15

NOUNS	VERBS	ADJECTIVES	ADVERB
calendar meeting	get	crazy	back
fish niece	go	sure	
French sandwich	plan	wrong	
(lang.) train	see (understand)		
lunch	show		
math	suppose		

GRAMMAR WORDS	EXPRESSIONS	NAMES
Contractions:	by the way	Masculine Names:
I'll we'll	have a party	Luis Phil
	have dinner	Place Names:
COMPOUNDS	Happy birthday!	Bangkok Madrid
	in an hour	Lisbon Paris
birthday party	the day after tomorrow	London Singapore
weekend	Tuesday of next week	Days of the Week:
	You're all wrong.	Sunday Thursday
		Monday Friday
		Wednesday

LESSON 16

DIALOGS: A DINNER PARTY

Dr. Garcia (Dr. G) and Dr. Baker (Dr. B) are at a dinner party. The party is for scientists attending an international scientific meeting. Dr. G and Dr. B discuss and identify various people in the room.

1

DR. G Isn't that Dr. Swenson from Sweden?

DR. B Yes, it is.
He's the famous chemist.

DR. G Where's he teaching now?

DR. B He's not teaching this year.
He's doing research.

2

DR. G That's Dr. Rodriguez.

DR. B From Mexico?

DR. G No, he's from Los Angeles.
He's American.

DR. B Oh, yes, now I remember.
He's giving a paper on genetics tomorrow.

3

DR. G That's Dr. Kimura.

DR. B I don't know him.

DR. G He's a very famous biologist.
He's doing research on heredity.

DR. B Where's he from?

DR. G From Osaka, Japan.

4

DR. G That's Dr. Weiss over there.

DR. B Dr. Hugo Weiss from Germany?

DR. G That's right. He's the famous physicist.

DR. B My, there are a lot of famous people here.

DR. G Yes, there certainly are.

126 | UNIT 4 LESSON 16

PRACTICE DRILLS AND EXERCISES (1)

1 Cities, Countries and Nationalities

Study this table.

CAPITAL CITY	COUNTRY	ADJECTIVE AND NATIONALITY
Rangoon	Burma	Burmese
Tokyo	Japan	Japanese
Peking	China	Chinese
Bangkok	Thailand	Thai
Seoul	Korea	Korean
Phnom Penh	Cambodia	Cambodian
Rome	Italy	Italian
Berlin	Germany	German
Oslo	Norway	Norwegian
Madrid	Spain	Spanish
Paris	France	French
Stockholm	Sweden	Swedish
Ottawa	Canada	Canadian
Washington, D.C.	the United States	American
Mexico City	Mexico	Mexican
Bogotá	Colombia	Colombian
Brasilia	Brazil	Brazilian
Caracas	Venezuela	Venezuelan

Repeat the words given. Then form sentences. Follow the models.

1. Rangoon Burma Burmese
   Rangoon's in Burma. It's a Burmese city.

2. Seoul Korea Korean
   Seoul's in Korea. It's a Korean city.

3. Rome Italy Italian
   ....

4. Berlin Germany German
   ....

5. Paris France French
   ....

6. Ottawa Canada Canadian
   ....

7. Bogotá Colombia Colombian
   ....

8. Caracas Venezuela Venezuelan
   ....

9. Amsterdam the Netherlands Dutch
   ....

2 Cities, Countries and Nationalities

Take the part of Speaker B.

ERIC WAS BORN IN STOCKHOLM.

SPEAKER A	What country is Eric from?
SPEAKER B	*He's from Sweden.*
SPEAKER A	What's his nationality?
SPEAKER B	*He's Swedish.*

MISS PEREZ WAS BORN IN BOGOTÁ.

SPEAKER A	What country is Miss Perez from?
SPEAKER B	....
SPEAKER A	What's her nationality?
SPEAKER B	....

JOHN WAS BORN IN OSLO.

SPEAKER A	What country is John from?
SPEAKER B	....
SPEAKER A	What's his nationality?
SPEAKER B	....

MISS DURAND WAS BORN IN PARIS.

SPEAKER A	What country is Miss Durand from?
SPEAKER B	....
SPEAKER A	What's her nationality?
SPEAKER B	....

HELEN AND JO WERE BORN IN OTTAWA.

SPEAKER A	What country are Helen and Jo from?
SPEAKER B	....
SPEAKER A	What's their nationality?
SPEAKER B	....

MRS. ODA WAS BORN IN TOKYO.

SPEAKER A	What country is Mrs. Oda from?
SPEAKER B	....
SPEAKER A	What's her nationality?
SPEAKER B	....

CHARLES WAS BORN IN WASHINGTON, D.C.

SPEAKER A	What country is Charles from?
SPEAKER B	....
SPEAKER A	What's his nationality?
SPEAKER B	....

UNIT 4 LESSON 16 | 129

LYDIA AND ANN WERE BORN IN MONTREAL.

SPEAKER A What country are Lydia and Ann from?
SPEAKER B ....
SPEAKER A What's their nationality?
SPEAKER B ....

3 Question-word (Wh-) Questions: Using *What* with Profession and Nationality

Take the part of Speaker B.

MR. CARLSON'S SWEDISH.

SPEAKER A Mr. Carlson isn't Norwegian.
SPEAKER B *What is he?*
SPEAKER A *He's Swedish.*

THEY'RE CHEMISTS.

SPEAKER A They aren't biologists.
SPEAKER B *What are they?*
SPEAKER A *They're chemists.*

MERCEDES IS MEXICAN.

SPEAKER A Mercedes isn't Brazilian.
SPEAKER B ....?
SPEAKER A ....

MISS DURAND'S A TEACHER.

SPEAKER A Miss Durand's not a secretary.
SPEAKER B ....?
SPEAKER A ....

HIS PARENTS ARE AMERICAN.

SPEAKER A His parents aren't Canadian.
SPEAKER B ....?
SPEAKER A ....

DR. BLACK'S A PROFESSOR.

SPEAKER A Dr. Black isn't a medical doctor.
SPEAKER B ....?
SPEAKER A ....

4 Conjunction (with Deletion): *and... too*

Construct the third sentence in each group. Follow the models.

1. Don's Canadian.
   Thomas is Canadian, too.
   Don's Canadian and Thomas is, too.

2. Mercedes is Mexican.
   Dolores is Mexican, too.
   Mercedes is Mexican and Dolores is, too.

3. Dr. Nelson was early.
   I was early, too.
   Dr. Nelson was early and I was, too.

4. He was reading.
   I was reading, too.

   ....

5. They were listening to the tape.
   We were listening to the tape, too.

   ....

6. He's Japanese.
   She's Japanese, too.

   ....

7. We're Swedish.
   They're Swedish, too.

   ....

8. They were on time.
   We were on time, too.

   ....

9. Miss Green was typing.
   I was typing, too.

   . . . .

10. Alice was walking home.
    Jim was walking home, too.

    . . . .

11. We were watching TV.
    Tom was watching TV, too.

    . . . .

DIALOGS FOR COMPREHENSION

Listen to these dialogs several times. Make sure you understand them. Learn the new words.

1

HELEN	Where were you yesterday, Ellie?
ELLIE	At the farm.
HELEN	What were you doing there?
ELLIE	Visiting my grandparents.
HELEN	Was it fun?
ELLIE	Oh, yes. It was lots of fun.

2

LUIS	What are we going to do tomorrow?
PHIL	I don't know. Let's play tennis.
LUIS	Okay. That's a good idea.

3

ELLIE   Was Lesson 16 hard?

HELEN   Yes, it was quite difficult.

ELLIE   Lesson 17 was hard, too.

HELEN   How was Lesson 18?

ELLIE   It was easy.
I like easy lessons.

4

MR. JAMES   Were you and the Carlsons at the party?

MR. WATSON   We were there, but they weren't.

5

LUIS   Were Lessons 12 and 13 easy?

PHIL   Well, Lesson 12 was easy, but Lesson 13 wasn't.

6

TED   Where's the calendar?

TOM   Right over there.

TED   What day is today?

TOM   It's Tuesday.
It's Tuesday, January 12.

TED   Well, tomorrow's a very important day.

TOM   Why?

TED   It's my birthday!

7

MR. WATSON   Let's go out to dinner tonight.
MRS. WATSON   Oh, fine! That's a good idea.

8

LARRY   Mommy, I'm hungry.
MRS. LOW   I'm cooking dinner, now, Larry.
LARRY   But I'm hungry, now.
MRS. LOW   All right. Here's a cookie. Now go and play.

PRACTICE DRILLS AND EXERCISES (2)

1   Suggestion: *Let's* + Verb

Repeat after Speaker A.

SPEAKER A	SPEAKER B
Let's go.	Okay.
Let's go to the movies.	That's a good idea.
Let's go out to dinner.	That's fine with me.
Let's go home now.	All right.

Take the part of Speaker A. Use the cue word and make a suggestion.

(CUE)	SPEAKER A	SPEAKER B
(WALK)	*Let's walk.*	All right.
(TAKE A WALK)	....	Good idea.
(WALK TO WORK)	....	Fine with me.
(EAT DINNER NOW)	....	All right. I'm hungry now.

(HAVE A PARTY)	....	Okay.
(GO FISHING)	....	That's a great idea!
(PLAY TENNIS TOMORROW)	....	Good idea. Let's go early.

2 Conjunction (with Deletion): *but*

Construct the third sentence in each group.

1. Tom isn't home.
   His brother's home.
   Tom isn't home, but his brother is. ....

2. He isn't French.
   She's French.
   He isn't French, but she is. ....

3. He wasn't from Italy.
   His friend was from Italy.
   ....

4. We were there last Thursday.
   They weren't there last Thursday.
   ....

5. Dr. Carlson isn't famous.
   Dr. Kimura's famous.
   ....

6. We weren't singing.
   They were singing.
   ....

7. He's not Spanish.
   They're Spanish.
   ....

UNIT 4 LESSON 16 | 135

8. He's writing a book.
   I'm not writing a book.

   . . . .

9. He was wrong.
   I wasn't wrong.

   . . . .

10. Lesson 17 was easy.
    Lesson 18 wasn't easy.

    . . . .

11. They weren't having fun.
    We were having fun.

    . . . .

12. They're going.
    We aren't going.

    . . . .

LISTENING PRACTICE: AFTER THE PARTY

After Alice's birthday party, Jim and Alice walk home together.

ALICE My, that was a nice party.
       Did you have a good time?

JIM   Yes, I did.
       You certainly have a lot of friends.

ALICE Thanks for the gift, Jim.
       I like books.

JIM   You're welcome.
       Say, let's play tennis tomorrow.

ALICE Fine. About eight o'clock?

JIM   Okay.

ALICE When are you going back to school, Jim?

JIM   Oh, in about ten days.

ALICE I'll miss you.*

JIM   I'll miss you too, Alice.

**I'll miss you* is a new vocabulary item. *To miss someone* is to feel sad because that person is not with you.

NEW VOCABULARY IN LESSON 16

NOUNS		VERB	ADJECTIVES	
country (nation)	Mommy parent	miss	American Burmese	French German
fun	physicist		Colombian	important
genetics	research		difficult	Italian
heredity	tennis		Dutch	medical
			famous	Venezuelan

COMPOUND

medical doctor

EXPRESSIONS

a great idea
a lot of
be fun
do research
give a paper
go fishing
have fun
I'll miss you.
lots of fun
play tennis
right there
You're welcome.

NAMES

Family:
  Durand   Low   Swenson
  Kimura   Rodriguez Weiss

Masculine:
  Charles Hugo
  Don   Larry

Feminine:
  Dolores Lydia
  Jo   Mercedes

Country:
  Colombia Italy   the Netherlands
  France   Mexico   Venezuela
  Germany

City:
  Amsterdam Los Angeles Rome
  Berlin   Osaka   Seoul
  Bogotá   Oslo   Stockholm
  Brasilia   Ottawa   Washington, D.C.
  Caracas   Rangoon

UNIT 5

THE PEOPLE IN UNIT 5

LAURA LARSON
(Mr. Watson's secretary)
Age 26
Single
Mr. Watson's personal
secretary at work

EDWARD YAMATO
(works with Mr. Watson)
Age 34
A scientist who works
in Mr. Watson's Division

ANITA LOPEZ
(friend of Alice Hayes)
Age 18
Friend and schoolmate
of Alice Hayes

UNIT 5 LESSON 17 | 139

LESSON 17

DIALOGS

Dialog 1: The Efficient Secretary

Mr. Watson is a biologist who works for the government. He is working in his office. His secretary, Miss Larson, knocks and enters.

(Miss Larson knocks)

MISS LARSON Excuse me, Mr. Watson.

MR. WATSON Yes? What is it?

MISS LARSON The staff meeting's at four.
You're going, aren't you?

MR. WATSON Yes, of course I'm going.
But it's only three now, isn't it?

MISS LARSON No. It's ten to four, Mr. Watson.

(Mr. Watson shakes his watch)

MR. WATSON Why, my watch isn't running!
I can't believe it.
Thank you, Miss Larson.

Dialog 2: At the Meeting

Mr. Watson enters the meeting room and sits down next to Mr. Edward Yamato. It's a few minutes after 4:00, but the meeting hasn't started yet. Dr. Lewis, chairman of the department, has not arrived.

MR. WATSON Hello, Ed.

MR. YAMATO Hello, Bob.
You're a little late, aren't you?

MR. WATSON Yes, my watch was slow.

MR. YAMATO	Well, it doesn't matter. Dr. Lewis isn't here yet.
MR. WATSON	Good. I need a few minutes to think.
MR. YAMATO	You're giving a report today, aren't you?
MR. WATSON	Yes, I am.
MR. YAMATO	Oh, here's Dr. Lewis. Good luck!

PRACTICE DRILLS AND EXERCISES (1)

1 Tag Questions: Intonation

Repeat these questions that have a negative tag.

QUESTION	EXPECTED ANSWER	POSSIBLE ANSWER
(FULL INTONATION MARKINGS)		
Ted's a lawyer, isn't he?	Yes, he is.	No, he isn't.
That's Ed, isn't it.	Yes, it is.	No, it isn't.
They're leaving, aren't they?	Yes, they are.	No, they aren't.
Tom and I are late, aren't we?	Yes, you are.	No, you aren't.
(ABBREVIATED INTONATION MARKINGS)		
You're going, aren't you?	Yes, I am.	No, I'm not.
We're on time, aren't we?	Yes, you are.	No, you're not.
That's your daughter, isn't it?	Yes, it is.	No, it isn't.
Miss Caine's your niece, isn't she?	Yes, she is.	No, she isn't.

2 Tag Questions: Negative Tag

Practice this conversation.

1. They're from Brazil, aren't they?
    Yes, they are.
    They're both Brazilian.
    He's from Rio.
    And she's from Recife.

2. You're from Central America, aren't you?
   Yes, I am.
   I'm from Honduras.

3. Carlos is from Central America too, isn't he?
   No, he's not.
   He's from South America.
   I think he's from Argentina.

3 Forming Tag Questions: Negative Tag with Affirmative Short Answers

Repeat the questions after Speaker A.

AFFIRMATIVE STATEMENT
1. TOM'S EARLY.
2. THOSE ARE HIS BOOKS.
3. IT'S NINE O'CLOCK.
4. THEY'RE CHINESE.

SPEAKER A	SPEAKER B
NEGATIVE TAG	EXPECTED SHORT ANSWER
1. Tom's early, isn't he?	Yes, he is.
2. Those are his books, aren't they?	Yes, they are.
3. It's nine o'clock, isn't it?	Yes, it is.
4. They're Chinese, aren't they?	Yes, they are.

Take the part of Speaker A. Form questions with negative tags.

AFFIRMATIVE STATEMENT
1. THEY're GOOD FRIENDS.
2. MARY'S ITALIAN.
3. WE'RE GOING.
4. ERIC'S FROM SWEDEN.
5. BOB'S AT THE MEETING.
6. ELLIE'S SLEEPING.
7. WE'RE ON TIME.

SPEAKER A NEGATIVE TAG	SPEAKER B EXPECTED SHORT ANSWER
1. *They're good friends, aren't they?*	Yes, they are.
2. ....?	Yes, she is.
3. ....?	Yes, we are.
4. ....?	Yes, he is.
5. ....?	Yes, he is.
6. ....?	Yes, she is.
7. ....?	Yes, we are.

4 Tag Questions: Negative Tag

Substitute the nationalities.

He's *English,* isn't he?

He's *Burmese,* isn't he? *(Burmese)*

.............................*(American)*

.............................*(Canadian)*

.............................*(Colombian)*

Substitute the subjects. Make necessary changes in the tags.

They're Brazilian, aren't they?

She's Brazilian, isn't she? .... *(She's)*

.............................*(John's)*

.............................*(Jane's)*

.............................*(You're)*

BASIC SENTENCES

Listen to these sentences. Then repeat them.

1. I like coffee.
2. I drink it every day.
3. I always have some for breakfast.
4. Sometimes I drink one cup of coffee.
5. Sometimes I have two cups.
6. I have it with sugar and cream.
7. I use two lumps of sugar.
8. And I take just a little bit of cream.  
9. My children like milk.
10. They have one or two glasses at every meal. 
11. My wife drinks tea.
12. She drinks it all day.
13. She drinks ten or twelve cups a day.

PRACTICE DRILLS AND EXERCISES (2)

1 Introduction to Mass Nouns: Liquids *(water/milk/tea/coffee/cream/fruit juice)*

Substitute the nouns.

There's some *milk* on the table.

There's some *water* on the table. *(water)*

.... *(tea)*

.... *(coffee)*

.... *(fruit juice)*

.... *(cream)*

Repeat these phrases.

glass of water   Here's a glass of water.

bottle of milk   Here's a bottle of milk.

cup of coffee   Here's a cup of coffee.

pot of tea   Here's a pot of tea.

glass of fruit juice   Here's a glass of fruit juice.

Repeat these phrases.

a glass of fresh milk

a cup of hot tea

a glass of cold water

a cup of black coffee

a glass of cold fruit juice

2 Mass Noun *water* with Definite and Indefinite Quantities

Repeat the sentences.

A. SOME = INDEFINITE QUANTITY

Please give me some water.

I want some water.

I want some water to drink.

I'm drinking some water.

I need some water for my car.

The children want some water.

B. GLASS OF = DEFINITE QUANTITY

I want a glass of water.

I'd like a glass of water, please.

May I have a glass of water?

This isn't a glass of water, is it?

Is that a full glass of water?

Are there two glasses of water there?

3 Count and Mass Nouns

Study this table.

	NOUN	INDEFINITE QUANTITY *some*	DEFINITE QUANTITY
COUNT NOUNS	pencil pen desk lawyer	*some* pencils *some* pens *some* desks *some* lawyers	*two* pencils *three* pens *six* desks *two* lawyers
MASS NOUNS	coffee milk tea water cream fruit juice	*some* coffee *some* milk *some* tea *some* water *some* cream *some* fruit juice	*two cups of* coffee *a glass of* milk *three pots of* tea *eight bottles of* water *two pints of* cream *six glasses of* fruit juice

Student 1: Use *some* with the noun given by the teacher.
Student 2: Give a definite quantity (more than one) of the noun given by the teacher. For mass nouns, use as appropriate *glass, cup, pot,* etc.

TEACHER	STUDENT 1	STUDENT 2
1. PENCIL	*some pencils*	*sixteen pencils*
2. COFFEE	*some coffee*	*three cups of coffee*
3. MAP	....	....
4. TEA	....	....
5. WATER	....	....

6. LETTER ....

7. CHILD ....

8. MILK ....

9. BOY ....

10. MAN ....

4 **Practice with Long Sentences**

Substitute the noun phrases.

I always drink *a cup of black coffee* for breakfast every morning.

I always drink *a glass of cold fruit juice* for breakfast every morning.

.... *(a cup of hot tea)* ....

.... *(a glass of cold milk)* ....

(two cups of coffee with cream and sugar) ....

NEW VOCABULARY IN LESSON 17

NOUNS		VERBS	ADJECTIVES		ADVERB
bit	lump	drink	Australian	fresh	sometimes
bottle	meal	need	black	cold	
breakfast	milk	run (of	Brazilian	hot	
car	pot	a watch)	efficient	slow	
coffee	sugar	think	English		
cup	water	use			
glass	tea				
cream	juice				
fruit					

EXPRESSIONS

give a report   It doesn't matter.
Good luck.   May I have . . . ?
I can't believe it.   Why!

GRAMMAR WORDS

Noun Determiner:
  some
Conjunction: or

COMPOUNDS

fruit juice
staff meeting

NAMES

Family:
  Caine
  Lewis
  Yamato
Masculine:
  Carlos
  Edward
Feminine:
  Laura

Places:
  Argentina
  Central America
  Honduras
  Recife
  Rio de Janeiro
  South America

LESSON 18

BASIC SENTENCES
Listen to these sentences. Then repeat them.

1. I'm a very fortunate person.
2. I'm fortunate because I have a lot of friends.
3. I was thinking the other day.
4. My friends do all kinds of work.
5. Walt Murray's an engineer.
6. His profession is engineering.
7. His field is engineering.
8. He's an electronics engineer.
9. Dick Stewart is a professor.
10. His profession is teaching.
11. His field is teaching or education.
12. He's a professor of education.
13. Mason Morley's a doctor.
14. His field is medicine.
15. He's a medical doctor.
16. Captain Strong's an army officer.
17. Al Parker's a civil engineer.
18. Jack Porter's a clerk.
19. He's with the government.
20. He's a clerk in the Department of Education.
21. Pamela Hudson's an artist.
22. She's quite a famous artist.
23. And what am I?
24. I'm an architect.

PRACTICE DRILLS AND EXERCISES (1)

1 Vocabulary: Professional Fields

Repeat these sentences.

A teacher is in the field of teaching.

A lawyer's in the field of law.

An engineer's in the field of engineering.

A doctor's in the field of medicine.

A nurse is in the field of nursing.

An architect's in the field of architecture.

An artist's in the field of art.

A professor's in the field of education.

2 Using *What* to Ask about Occupation, Nationality and Position

Take the part of Speaker A.

STATEMENT OF FACT
OCCUPATION
1. TED'S AN ENGINEER.
2. JANE'S AN ARTIST.
NATIONALITY
3. MARIA'S SPANISH.
4. ERIC'S SWEDISH.
POSITION
5. MR. CHANG'S THE PRESIDENT.
6. MR. LOW'S THE VICE-PRESIDENT.

SPEAKER A	SPEAKER B
WH- QUESTION	COMPLETE ANSWER
(*Use* what)	
OCCUPATION	
1. *What's Ted?*	He's an engineer.
2. ....?	She's an artist.

150 | UNIT 5 LESSON 18

NATIONALITY

3. ....? She's Spanish.

4. ....? He's Swedish.

POSITION

5. ....? He's the president.

6. ....? He's the vice-president.

Take the part of Speaker B. Give complete answers. Use pronoun subjects.

STATEMENT OF FACT

1. MR. WATSON'S A SCIENTIST.
2. MRS. WATSON'S A NURSE.
3. MR. BELLINI'S ITALIAN.
4. MR. JENNINGS IS THE PRESIDENT.
5. MRS. KELLY'S IRISH.

SPEAKER A
WH- QUESTION

SPEAKER B
COMPLETE ANSWER

1. What's Mr. Watson? ....
2. What's Mrs. Watson? ....
3. What's Mr. Bellini? ....
4. What's Mr. Jennings? ....
5. What's Mrs. Kelly? ....

UNIT 5 LESSON 18 | 151

3 Tag Questions: Negative Statement with Affirmative Tag

Take the part of Student A. Form tag questions with rising intonation.

	NEGATIVE STATEMENT	SPEAKER A AFFIRMATIVE TAG	SPEAKER B EXPECTED SHORT ANSWER
1.	TED ISN'T HERE.	*Ted isn't here, is he?*	No, he isn't.
2.	THAT ISN'T ALICE.	.................?	No, it isn't.
3.	WE AREN'T LATE.	.................?	No, we're not.
4.	SHE'S NOT CANADIAN.	.................?	No, she isn't.
5.	MARY'S NOT AN ARTIST.	.................?	No, she's not.
6.	THEY'RE NOT MARRIED.	.................?	No, they aren't.
7.	IT ISN'T NOON.	.................?	No, it isn't.
8.	YOU AND TOM AREN'T GOING.	.................?	No, we aren't.
9.	HE'S NOT A CIVIL ENGINEER.	.................?	No, he's not.
10.	MR. LING ISN'T ITALIAN.	.................?	No, he's not.

DIALOGS

Listen to these conversations. Then repeat.

Dialog 1

It's morning in the Watson household.

MR. WATSON   Is breakfast ready?

MRS. WATSON   Yes, it's on the table.

MR. WATSON   Mmmmm. French toast! May I have the jelly, please?

MRS. WATSON   Isn't it on the table? No, here it is.

MR. WATSON   Wow!

MRS. WATSON   What's the matter?

MR. WATSON   This coffee's hot!

Dialog 2

It's still morning in the Watson household.

MRS. WATSON Are you ready for breakfast, Ellie?
ELLIE Yes. I want a bowl of cereal, and some toast.
MRS. WATSON The cereal's on the table. And I'm making some toast now.
ELLIE The butter isn't on the table.
MRS. WATSON I have it here. And here's the cream and sugar for your cereal.

Dialog 3

It's afternoon in the Watson household.

TOMMY I'm hungry, Mom. May I have a piece of bread?
MRS. WATSON Tommy, what's that all over your clothes? Why, it's chalk.
TOMMY It is?
MRS. WATSON And look at your hands. They're dirty.
TOMMY They are?
MRS. WATSON Now you go upstairs. And wash with soap, young man.

PRACTICE DRILLS AND EXERCISES (2)

1 **Mass Nouns: Using *some* to Indicate an Indefinite Amount**
   Foods: *bread/toast/French toast/butter/jelly/cereal*
   Other: *chalk/soap*

   Repeat. Pronounce *some* with weak stress.

some bread	some milk
some toast	some cereal
some jelly	some bread and butter

   Substitute the noun phrases.

   May I have *some bread*, please?
   May I have *some toast*, please? *(some toast)*
   .... *(some butter)*
   .... *(some jelly)*
   .... *(some cereal)*

   Repeat these sentences.

   Mother's making some bread.
   Ellie's making some toast for us.
   Please have some jelly.
   I'd like some cereal, please.
   There's some chalk on the table.
   Get some soap at the store.

2 **Mass Nouns: Expressing Definite Quantities**

   Repeat the words and phrases.

   bread
     loaf
     loaves *(pl.)*

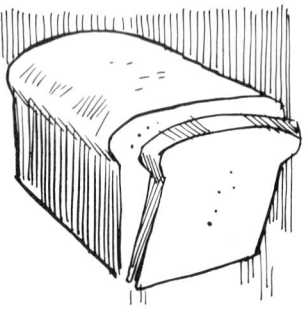

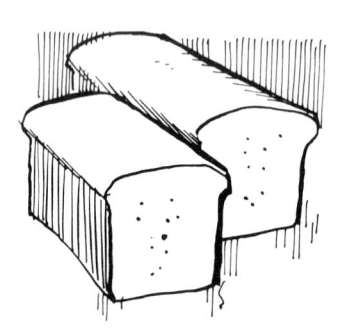

   a loaf of bread   two loaves of bread

bread
piece
slice

a piece of bread

four slices of bread

toast
piece

a piece of toast

coffee
cup

two cups of coffee

butter
cube
stick
pound

a stick of butter
a cube of butter

two pounds of butter

jelly
jar

a jar of jelly

two jars of jelly

UNIT 5 LESSON 18 | 155

cereal
bowl
box

a bowl of cereal

two boxes of cereal

chalk
piece

a piece of chalk

two pieces of chalk

soap
bar
cake

a bar of soap
a cake of soap

three bars of soap
three cakes of soap

paper
piece
sheet

a piece of paper

two sheets of paper

Repeat these sentences.

We need a loaf of white bread.
Get two loaves of bread at the store.
That's certainly a big piece of bread!
I'd like two pieces of French toast, please.
Get two sticks of butter at the store.
This is a new jar of jelly, isn't it?
I eat two bowls of cereal for breakfast.
I need a piece of yellow chalk.
This is my last sheet of paper.

3 Count and Mass Nouns: Definite and Indefinite Quantities

Student 1: Use *some* with the noun supplied by the teacher.
Student 2: Give a definite quantity (more than one) of the noun. For mass nouns, use as appropriate *glass, cup, piece*, etc.

	TEACHER	STUDENT 1	STUDENT 2
1.	GIRL	*some girls*	*four girls*
2.	TOAST	*some toast*	*two pieces of toast*
3.	SOAP	....	....
4.	CLOCK	....	....
5.	COFFEE	....	....
6.	FARMER	....	....
7.	GLASS	....	....
8.	TEA	....	....
9.	BUTTER	....	....
10.	NURSE	....	....
11.	CITY	....	....
12.	BREAD	....	....
13.	JELLY	....	....
14.	CUP	....	....
15.	WATER	....	....

NEW VOCABULARY IN LESSON 18

NOUNS			VERB
architect	education	paper	wash
architecture	electronics	piece	
bar (of soap)	engineering	pound	
bowl	field	profession	ADJECTIVES
box	(occupation)	sheet	
bread	hand	(of paper)	dirty
butter	household	slice	fortunate
cake (of soap)	jar	soap	white
captain	jelly	stick (of butter)	yellow
cereal	kind	store	
chalk	loaf	teaching	
clerk	loaves (pl.)	toast	
cube (of butter)	medicine	vice-president	
department	officer		

GRAMMAR WORDS	EXPRESSIONS	NAMES

Noun Determiner:
  other
Subordinator:
  because
	all kinds
	all over
	civil engineer
	French toast
	Mmm!
		Family:
		  Bellini Mason Parker
		  Hudson Morley Stewart
		  Jennings Murray Strong
		  Kelly

COMPOUNDS	the other day What's the matter? Wow!	Masculine: Al Tommy Dick Walt Feminine: Pamela
army officer white bread		

LESSON 19

READING: A LETTER TO JIM

During the summer, Jim Carter became good friends with Alice Hayes. Jim is now back at the University of Chicago, but he and Alice write frequently. This is a letter that Alice wrote him.

Madison, Wisconsin
November 18, 1975

Dear Jim,

I was very glad to hear from you. I'm glad that you are doing so well in all your subjects.

I was late for my first class today. Let me tell you about it. I'm always on time for class. At least I try to be. But this morning at half past eight I was looking for my shoe. One shoe was in my room but the other was missing. At nine o'clock my little sister was going past my door. Guess what was on her foot. My missing shoe! She was playing with it.

I was late for school, but the teacher wasn't upset. She was very nice about it. Actually, she's always nice. I guess we all have our troubles.

Anita wants to go to a movie tonight, but I'm not going. I have a lot of homework.

I miss you very much, so please write again soon.

Love,
Alice

UNIT 5 LESSON 19 | 159

PRACTICE DRILLS AND EXERCISES (1)

1   Possessive Determiners: *my/your/his/her/our/their* **(New Vocabulary)**

Repeat these tag questions.

That's my hat, isn't it?

Those are your hats, aren't they?

That's her coat, isn't it?

Those are her stockings, aren't they?

These are his shirts, aren't they?

Those are his socks, aren't they?

That's my shoe, isn't it?

Repeat the answers given by Speaker B.

A What are you looking for?
B I'm looking for my shirt.

A What's Alice looking for?
B She's looking for her shoe.

A What's Tommy looking for?
B He's looking for his socks.

A What are you looking for?
B We're looking for our coats.

A What are they looking for?
B They're looking for their hats.

Substitute the pronoun subjects. Use the possessive form that corresponds with the subject of the sentence.

She isn't taking care of *her* children.
You aren't taking care of *your* children. *(You ... your)*

.... *(He ... his)*
.... *(We ... our)*
.... *(They ... their)*
.... *(I ... my)*

Substitute the pronoun subjects. Again, use the possessive form that corresponds with the subject. Change the tag ending as needed.

They're writing their report, aren't they?
He's writing his report, isn't he? *(He ... his)*
.... *(We ... our)*
.... *(She ... her)*
.... *(You ... your)*

2 Asking about Age: *How old?*

Take the part of Speaker B. Give complete answers using pronoun subjects.

STATEMENT OF FACT
1. ELLIE WATSON'S TEN YEARS OLD.
2. TOMMY'S FOUR.
3. JIM CARTER'S TWENTY YEARS OLD.
4. MR. LING'S THIRTY-SEVEN YEARS OLD.
5. ELLIE'S GRANDFATHER IS ABOUT SIXTY.
6. MR. SMITH IS THIRTY-SIX.

	SPEAKER A WH- QUESTION*	SPEAKER B COMPLETE ANSWER
1.	How old's Ellie Watson?	*She's ten years old.*
2.	How old's Tommy?	*He's four.*
3.	How old's Jim Carter?	....
4.	How old's Mr. Ling?	....
5.	How old's Ellie's grandfather?	....
6.	How old's Mr. Smith?	....

*Although the question word *How* does not begin with *Wh-*, it functions as other Wh- question words. Consequently, we classify questions with *How* as Wh- questions.

Take the part of Speaker A. Form question-word questions.

	STATEMENT OF FACT
1.	KATHY'S TEN.
2.	IRENE LING'S TWENTY-EIGHT.
3.	ALICE HAYES IS 18 YEARS OLD.
4.	MY FRIEND'S ABOUT 40.
5.	DR. HAMM'S FIFTY YEARS OLD.
6.	THE CHILDREN ARE TWELVE.

SPEAKER A   SPEAKER B
WH- QUESTION   COMPLETE ANSWER

1. ....?   She's ten.
2. ....?   She's twenty-eight.
3. ....?   She's 18 years old.
4. ....?   He's about forty.
5. ....?   He's fifty years old.
6. ....?   They're twelve.

QUESTIONS AND ANSWERS

Listen to these questions and answers. Then repeat them.

1. Is there a good program on TV tonight?
    Yes, there is.
    It's a new movie.
    Let's look at it together.

2. Is there an eraser in the desk?
    I don't know.
    Let me look.
    Yes, there is one.

3. Are there two file clerks in your office?
    No, there aren't.
    There's only one.

4. There isn't any coffee, is there?
    No, there isn't.
    I'm sorry.

5. There are 30 students in your class, aren't there?
　　No, there aren't.
　　There are only 28.

6. How many offices are there in your building?
　　Oh, I don't know.
　　There are about forty, I guess.

7. How many cities are there in your country?
　　I have no idea.
　　There are hundreds.
　　Perhaps thousands.

PRACTICE DRILLS AND EXERCISES (2)

1 *There is/there are:* with Definite Quantities

Substitute the noun phrases.

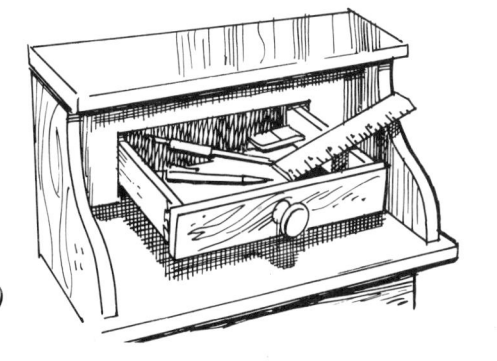

COUNT NOUNS

Singular: a = one

There's *a pencil* in the desk.
There's *a ruler* in the desk. *(a ruler)*
.... *(a pen)*
.... *(an eraser)*

MASS NOUNS

Singular: a = one

There's *a pot of tea* on the table.
There's *a cup of coffee* on the table.
.... *(a bowl of cereal)* ....
.... *(a glass of milk)* ....

UNIT 5 LESSON 19 | 165

COUNT NOUNS

Plural: 2, 3, 4, 5, etc.

There are *two secretaries* in our office.
There are *three typists* in our office. *(three typists)*

.... *(two file clerks)*

.... *(three clerks)*

MASS NOUNS

Plural: 2, 3, 4, 5, etc.

There are *two pots of coffee* in the kitchen.
There are *two boxes of cereal* in the kitchen. *(two boxes of cereal)*

.... *(four glasses of milk)*

.... *(two bowls of sugar)*

2 There is/there are: Yes/No Questions and Short Answers

Repeat the questions after Speaker A.

STATEMENT OF FACT
1. THERE'S A GOOD PROGRAM ON TV.
2. THERE ARE 2 RADIOS IN HIS ROOM.
3. THERE'S A PEN IN THE DESK.
4. THERE ARE 30 STUDENTS HERE TODAY.
5. THERE ARE 2 WINDOWS IN THIS ROOM.
6. THERE'S A POT OF COFFEE IN THE KITCHEN.

SPEAKER A	SPEAKER B
YES/NO QUESTION	SHORT ANSWER
1. Is there a good program on TV?	Yes, there is.
2. Are there 2 radios in his room?	Yes, there are.
3. Is there a pen in the desk?	Yes, there is.
4. Are there 30 students here today?	Yes, there are.
5. Are there 2 windows in this room?	Yes, there are.
6. Is there a pot of coffee in the kitchen?	Yes, there is.

3 *There is/there are:* **Short Answers**

Repeat after Speaker B.

SPEAKER A   Is there a good movie in town?
SPEAKER B   No, there isn't.

SPEAKER A   Are there two secretaries in your office?
SPEAKER B   No, there aren't.

SPEAKER A   Is there a good program on TV tonight?
SPEAKER B   No, there isn't.

SPEAKER A   Are there three letters on the desk?
SPEAKER B   No, there aren't. There are only two.

(TAG QUESTIONS)
SPEAKER A   There's a famous artist in town, isn't there?
SPEAKER B   Yes, there is.

SPEAKER A   There are six visitors here today, aren't there?
SPEAKER B   Yes, there are.

SPEAKER A   There isn't a letter for me, is there?
SPEAKER B   No, there isn't.

SPEAKER A   There aren't two windows in that room, are there?
SPEAKER B   No, there aren't.

NEW VOCABULARY IN LESSON 19

NOUNS			VERBS	ADVERBS
country (nation)	kitchen love	sock stocking	hear write	actually perhaps
door	program	subject		soon
eraser	ruler	(course)	ADJECTIVE	together
foot	shirt	window		
hat	shoe		missing	

GRAMMAR WORDS	EXPRESSIONS	NAME
Question Words: how many how (+ adj.) Subordinator: so	at least be upset Dear (+Name), have no idea hundreds thousands	Family Name: Hamm
		COMPOUNDS file clerk homework

168 | UNIT 5 LESSON 19

LESSON 20

DIALOGS FOR COMPREHENSION

Listen to these dialogs several times. Make sure you understand them. Learn the new words.

Dialog 1: Getting Lunch

Mr. Watson telephoned and said he would be home for lunch. This was unusual. Mrs. Watson is hurrying to get things ready.

MRS. WATSON	Ellie, help me with the lunch, please. Your father's coming home this noon.
ELLIE	All right, Mother.
MRS. WATSON	Is there any tea in the cupboard?
ELLIE	Just a little. There's a full jar of instant coffee.
MRS. WATSON	That's fine. How much bread is there in the breadbox?
ELLIE	There's one loaf of white.
MRS. WATSON	Okay. Thank you. I guess we'll have soup, a sandwich, and coffee.
ELLIE	I'll set the table.
MRS. WATSON	That's a good girl. Thank you.

UNIT 5 LESSON 20 | 169

Dialog 2: Lunch is Served

It's a few minutes later and Mr. Watson comes in.

MR. WATSON	Hello, girls.
MRS. WATSON	Hello, dear.
ELLIE	Hi, Dad.
MR. WATSON	Where's Tommy?
MRS. WATSON	He's eating with Johnny today.
MR. WATSON	Is lunch ready?
MRS. WATSON	Yes, it's all ready.
ELLIE	Sit down, Daddy.
MR. WATSON	Mmmm. WOW! This soup's hot!

PRACTICE DRILLS AND EXERCISES (1)

1   *There is/there are:* **with Indefinite Quantities**

   Repeat the words and sentences on the next page.

COUNT NOUNS	MASS NOUNS
	Affirmative *some*
nurse	*milk*
There are some fine nurses here.	There's some milk in the kitchen.
worker	*chalk*
There are some good workers in our office.	There's some chalk in that box.
	Negative *any*
cup	*sugar*
There aren't any cups.	There isn't any sugar in this bowl.
letter	*bread*
There aren't any letters on her desk.	There isn't any bread.

2 *There is/there are:* **Question-word (Wh-) Questions with** *How many?*

Take the part of Speaker A.

STATEMENT OF FACT

1. THERE ARE TWO BOOKS.
2. THERE'S A RULER.
3. THERE ARE TWO GLASSES OF MILK.
4. THERE'S ONE SECRETARY.
5. THERE ARE THIRTY VISITORS.
6. THERE'S ONE STUDENT.
7. THERE ARE SIX GLASSES.
8. THERE'S ONE BOWL.
9. THERE ARE THREE MAPS.
10. THERE ARE SIXTY NURSES.

SPEAKER A WH- QUESTION	SPEAKER B
1. How many books are there?	There are two.
2. How many rulers are there?	There's one.
3. How many glasses of milk are there?	There are two.
4. How many secretaries are there?	There's one.
5. ....?	There are thirty.

UNIT 5 LESSON 20 | 171

6. ....? There's one.
7. ....? There are six.
8. ....? There's one.
9. ....? There are three.
10. ....? There are sixty.

3 There is/there are: Yes/No Questions with *any* and Short Answers

Repeat the questions after Speaker A.

STATEMENT OF FACT
1. THERE'S SOME COFFEE.
2. THERE ARE SOME QUESTIONS.
3. THERE'S SOME TEA IN THE POT.
4. THERE ARE SOME TAPES ON THE DESK.

SPEAKER A YES/NO QUESTION (*Use* any)	SPEAKER B SHORT ANSWER
1. Is there any coffee?	Yes, there is.
2. Are there any questions?	Yes, there are.
3. Is there any tea in the pot?	Yes, there is.
4. Are there any tapes on the desk?	Yes, there are.

Repeat the short answers after Speaker B.

NEGATIVE STATEMENT OF FACT	SPEAKER A YES/NO QUESTION (*Use* any)	SPEAKER B SHORT ANSWER
1. THERE ISN'T ANY SUGAR.	Is there any sugar?	No, there isn't.
2. THERE AREN'T ANY CUPS.	Are there any cups?	No, there aren't.
3. THERE ISN'T ANY BREAD.	Is there any bread?	No, there isn't.
4. THERE AREN'T ANY BOWLS.	Are there any bowls?	No, there aren't.

4 **Forming Question-word (Wh-) Questions with Mass Nouns:** *How much?*

Take the part of Speaker A. Form Wh- questions with cue words given by the teacher.

TEACHER		
1. MILK	5.	INSTANT COFFEE
2. RICE IN THE BOX	6.	BREAD IN THE BREADBOX
3. TEA IN THE POT	7.	BUTTER
4. SUGAR IN THE BOWL	8.	JELLY IN THAT JAR

SPEAKER A	SPEAKER B
WH- QUESTION	SHORT ANSWER
1. *How much milk is there?*	Very little.
2. *How much rice is there in the box?*	Not very much.
3. *How much tea is there in the pot?*	Not very much.
4. ....?	Very little.
5. ....?	Just a little.
6. ....?	Very little.
7. ....?	Not very much.
8. ....?	Just a little.

5 **Forming Question-word (Wh-) Questions with Count Nouns:** *How many?*

Take the part of Speaker A. Form Wh- questions from the cue expressions.

TEACHER		
1. BOYS IN THE CLASS	5.	FISH IN THE LAKE
2. TAPES ON THE DESK	6.	WOMEN AT THE PARTY
3. VISITORS IN THE OFFICE	7.	CUPS ON THE TABLE
4. MAPS ON THE WALL		

| SPEAKER A | SPEAKER B |
| WH- QUESTION | SHORT ANSWER |

1. *How many boys are there in the class?*   Very few.
2. *How many tapes are there on the desk?*   Only a few.
3. ....?   Just a few.
4. ....?   Only one.
5. ....?   Not very many.
6. ....?   Only a few.
7. ....?   Four or five.

QUESTIONS AND ANSWERS

Listen to these questions and answers. Then repeat them.

1. You weren't here Friday, were you?
    No, I wasn't.
    I was here Wednesday and Thursday.
    But I wasn't here Friday.

2. You were out of town, weren't you?
    Yes, I was.
    I was in Chicago.
    There was an important meeting there.

3. You weren't born in Argentina, were you?
    No, I wasn't.
    I was born in Valparaiso.

4. That's in Chile, isn't it?
    That's right.
    It's near Santiago.

5. That wasn't your daughter, was it?
    Oh, my, no!
    That was my sister.

6. Your wife wasn't upset, was she?
    Because I was late last night?
    Oh, no.
    She wasn't angry at all.

7. Was the movie good?
    Yes, it was.
    It was excellent.

8. Were there many people there?
    Yes, there were.
    The movie was full.

9. You were in the hospital, weren't you?
    Yes, I was there last week.

10. Were there any nice nurses?
    Of course.
    They were all nice.

11. You're not kidding me, are you?
    Now you know me better than that!

PRACTICE DRILLS AND EXERCISES (2)

1 Tag Questions: Past Tense Forms

Repeat after Speaker A.

SPEAKER A	SPEAKER B
Yesterday was a fine day, wasn't it?	Yes, it was.
Alice was looking for her shoe, wasn't she?	Yes, she was.
They weren't speaking English, were they?	No, they weren't.
That was your sister, wasn't it?	Yes, it was.
We were a little early, weren't we?	No, we weren't.
Lesson 22 was easy, wasn't it?	Yes, it was.
You weren't in Rome last week, were you?	No, I wasn't.

Substitute the subjects. Change the tag question as required.

SPEAKER A	SPEAKER B
She was speaking English, *wasn't she?*	Yes, she was.
He was speaking English, *wasn't he?* (He)	Yes, he was.
................................(We)	Yes, we were.
................................(Mrs. Kao)	Yes, she was.
................................(Mr. and Mrs. Low)	Yes, they were.

UNIT 5 LESSON 20 | 175

Take the part of Speaker A. Complete the sentences.

SPEAKER A	SPEAKER B
That wasn't your wife, ...?	No, ...
You were home last night, ...?	Yes, ...
They weren't army officers, ...?	No, ...
It was Tuesday, ...?	Yes, ...
Mary was watching TV, ...?	Yes, ...
Bill wasn't a medical student, ...?	No, ...
Mr. and Mrs. Ling weren't there, ...?	No, ...
Ellie was helping her mother, ...?	Yes, ...
I wasn't very upset, ...?	Yes, ...
Mr. Watson was walking to work, ...?	Yes, ...

2 *There is/there are* and *there was/there were:* **Tag Questions**

Speaker A: Fill in the blank and read the sentence.
Speaker B: Give the expected short answer.

SPEAKER A	SPEAKER B
1. There weren't many people at the meeting, *were there?*	*No, there weren't.*
2. There wasn't time to write my report, *was there?*	*No, there wasn't.*
3. There's a good hotel here, *isn't there?*	*Yes, there is.*
4. There's some coffee in the kitchen, ...?	....
5. There were four students absent today, ...?	....
6. There's some soup, ...?	....
7. There aren't any questions, ...?	....
8. There were some nice pictures in his office, ...?	....

9. There wasn't time, ...? ....
10. There isn't any cereal, ...? ....
11. There were some letters on the table, ...? ....
12. There weren't any letters for me, ...? ....
13. There are some good programs on TV, ...? ....

3 *There was/there were:* Short Answers

Speaker A: Fill in the blanks with *was, wasn't, were, weren't, any, much* or *there*.
Speaker B: Give a *yes* or *no* short answer.

SPEAKER A | SPEAKER B

1. There ..... some instant coffee, wasn't there? *Yes, there was.*
2. ..... there any women at the meeting? *Yes, there were a few.*
3. There wasn't time to read the letter, was .....? *No, there wasn't.*
4. There wasn't ..... coffee on the table, was there? ....
5. ..... there any sugar in the cupboard? ....
6. ..... there any chalk in the box? ....
7. ..... there any pencils on the desk? ....
8. There weren't any cups on the table, ... there? ....
9. ..... there many cups on the table? ....
10. There ..... any pens on the desk, ...? ....
11. ..... there ..... soup in the bowl? ....
12. There ..... some butter on the table, ...? ....

UNIT 5 LESSON 20 | 177

LISTENING PRACTICE: ALICE AND ANITA

Alice is walking along the street reading a letter. Her friend Anita sees her and stops to talk.

ANITA   What are you reading, Alice?
ALICE   Oh, hi, Anita. I'm reading a letter.
ANITA   From Jim?
ALICE   That's right.
ANITA   How is he?
ALICE   Oh, he's fine.
He's doing fine in all his subjects.
ANITA   What's he taking this year?
ALICE   Biology, chemistry, economics and history.
ANITA   Is he coming back to Madison soon?
ALICE   Yes, he's coming in December.
ANITA   Well, tell him hello for me.

ALICE	All right. We're still going to the movie tonight, aren't we?
ANITA	Yes. I'll be at your house at 7:30.
ALICE	Oh, my watch isn't running. What time is it now?
ANITA	Let's see. It's exactly ten after five.
ALICE	Oh, I'm late. Good-bye. I'll see you tonight, Anita.
ANITA	Okay. Good-bye.

NEW VOCABULARY IN LESSON 20

NOUNS			ADJECTIVE
biology	Dad	rice	angry
chemistry	Daddy	soup	
cupboard	economics	worker	

GRAMMAR WORD	EXPRESSIONS	NAMES

Question Word:
  how much
	be any good
	be served
	better than
		Family Name:
		  Kao
		Masculine Name:

COMPOUNDS	instant coffee out of town	Johnny Feminine Name:

breadbox
medical student
	set the table
	south of
	take (a course)
	You're not kidding me.
		Anita
		Place Names:
		  Chile
		  Santiago
		  Valparaiso

UNIT 6

LESSON 21

DIALOG: SURPRISING NEWS

Mr. Watson comes home about 4:00. He usually doesn't arrive home until about 5:30. He comes in the door and Mrs. Watson greets him.

(front door closes)

MR. WATSON	Hi, Barb.
MRS. WATSON	Hello, dear. You're home early.
MR. WATSON	Yes, a little bit. Guess what?
MRS. WATSON	What?
MR. WATSON	I'm going to attend the regional meeting.
MRS. WATSON	Oh, Bob, how nice! Where is it? And when is it? Next month?
MR. WATSON	It's in Miami. And it's tomorrow.

MRS. WATSON	Tomorrow!
MR. WATSON	Yes. Ed's sick and can't go. I'm going to report on my experiment.
MRS. WATSON	Tomorrow? When are you going to leave?
MR. WATSON	Tonight. I'm going to take the eight p.m. flight.
MRS. WATSON	Well, what a surprise! Come on. Let's hurry.

PRACTICE DRILLS AND EXERCISES (1)

1 Pronunciation: *going to* + Verb

Read across. Read the phrase and then the sentence. Then repeat.

going to leave	I'm going to leave soon.
going to call	He's going to call us.
going to walk	We're going to walk today.
going to drive	Jim's going to drive here.
going to sing	She's going to sing now.

2 *Going to* Future: Affirmative

Follow the models. Take the part of Speaker A.

1. TAKE A TRIP

   A *Guess what?* . . . .
   B *What?* . . . .
   A *I'm going to take a trip.* . . . . . .

2. WORK AT AN AIRLINE

   A *Guess what?* . . . .
   B *What?* . . . .
   A *I'm going to work at an airline.*

UNIT 6 LESSON 21 | 181

3. BUY A COLOR TV

    A   *Guess what?* ....

    B   ....?

    A   ....

4. GO TO THE FAR EAST

    A   ....?

    B   ....?

    A   ....

5. GET MARRIED SOON

    A   ....?

    B   ....?

    A   ....

6. REPORT ON MY EXPERIMENT

    A   ....?

    B   ....?

    A   ....

7. HAVE LUNCH WITH MARY

    A   ....?

    B   ....?

    A   ....

8. BUY A NEW CAR

    A   ....?

    B   ....?

    A   ....

3 *Going to* Future: Yes/No Questions

Repeat the yes/no questions after Speaker A.

	STATEMENT OF FACT
1.	HE'S GOING TO WALK.
2.	THEY'RE GOING TO LEAVE.
3.	SHE'S GOING TO LOOK AT TV.
4.	WE'RE GOING TO HAVE LUNCH NOW.

SPEAKER A — YES/NO QUESTION	SPEAKER B — AFFIRMATIVE SHORT ANSWER
1. Is he going to walk?	Yes, he is.
2. Are they going to leave?	Yes, they are.
3. Is she going to look at TV?	Yes, she is.
4. Are we going to have lunch now?	Yes, we are.

Take the part of Speaker A. Form yes/no questions.

	STATEMENT OF FACT
1.	HE'S GOING TO GO TO THE HOTEL.
2.	THEY'RE GOING TO EAT NOW.
3.	MARY'S GOING TO WALK HOME.
4.	IT'S GOING TO BE A SURPRISE.
5.	TED'S GOING TO STUDY ART.

SPEAKER A — YES/NO QUESTION	SPEAKER B — AFFIRMATIVE SHORT ANSWER
1. .... ?	Yes, he is.
2. .... ?	Yes, they are.
3. .... ?	Yes, she is.
4. .... ?	Yes, it is.
5. .... ?	Yes, he is.

4 *Going to* Future: Negative Forms

Read across. Repeat the phrase and then the sentence. Then repeat.

isn't going to call   He isn't going to call today.
aren't going to come   They aren't going to come tomorrow.
not going to have lunch   I'm not going to have lunch there.
aren't going to eat dinner We aren't going to eat dinner today.

5 *Going to* Future: Negative Statements and Echo Questions to Show Surprise

Speaker A: Make a negative statement. Use *isn't* or *aren't*. Use the word in parentheses as the subject.

Speaker B: Respond with a short negative form with rising intonation.

1. DRIVE TODAY (HE)

    SPEAKER A   *He isn't going to drive today.*
    SPEAKER B   *He isn't?*

2. BUY A COLOR TV (MISS GREEN)

    SPEAKER A   *Miss Green isn't going to buy a color TV.*
    SPEAKER B   *She isn't?*

3. BUY A NEW SUIT (TOM)

    SPEAKER A   ....
    SPEAKER B   ....?

4. GO TO WORK TODAY (MR. SMITH)

    SPEAKER A   ....
    SPEAKER B   ....?

5. TAKE A CAB (MRS. WATSON)

    SPEAKER A   ....
    SPEAKER B   ....?

6. ATTEND THE MEETING (WE)

   SPEAKER A   ....
   SPEAKER B   ....?

7. COME TOMORROW (TED AND MARY)

   SPEAKER A   ....
   SPEAKER B   ....?

8. HAVE LUNCH THERE (THEY)

   SPEAKER A   ....
   SPEAKER B   ....?

9. WORK ON THE EXPERIMENT (YOU AND I)

   SPEAKER A   ....
   SPEAKER B   ....?

DIALOG: GETTING READY FOR THE TRIP

Mrs. Watson is helping her husband get ready to catch the 8:00 p.m. flight. The dialog begins when Mr. Watson is going to make a telephone call.

MRS. WATSON	What are you doing?
MR. WATSON	I'm going to call a cab.
MRS. WATSON	No, you're not. I'm going to drive you.
MR. WATSON	But what about the children?
MRS. WATSON	Oh, Alice is going to take care of them. She's going to do her homework here.
MR. WATSON	Oh, fine. But it's getting late. It's 7:10 now.
	(the doorbell rings)
MRS. WATSON	There's the bell. That's Alice now.

UNIT 6 LESSON 21 | 185

PRACTICE DRILLS AND EXERCISES (2)

1 *Going to* **Future: Sentence Practice**

   Repeat these build-ups.

   1.   at twelve today

          lunch at twelve today

          have lunch at twelve today

     We're going to have lunch at twelve today.

   2.   to eat

          going to eat

          are you going to eat

     What are you going to eat?

   3.   soup

          some soup

          have some soup

          I'm going to have some soup

     I think I'm going to have some soup.

   4.   a sandwich

          have a sandwich

          going to have a sandwich

     Aren't you going to have a sandwich?

5.   by 4 o'clock

        hungry by 4 o'clock

           going to be hungry by 4 o'clock

You're going to be hungry by 4 o'clock.

6.   at four

        have tea at four

           going to have tea at four

We're going to have tea at four.

7.   at six

        eat dinner at six

           going to eat dinner at six

I'm going to eat dinner at six.

8.   fat

        get fat

You're not going to get fat.

9.   like my father

        be thin like my father

I'm going to be thin like my father.

10.   lunch

        lunch now

           going to go to lunch now

Well, I'm going to go to lunch now.

Listen to this dialog.

A I'm going to have lunch at twelve today.

B What are you going to eat?

A I'm going to have some soup.

B Aren't you going to have a sandwich?
You're going to be hungry by 4 o'clock.

A I'm going to have tea at four.
And I'm going to eat dinner at six.

B Well, you're not going to get fat.

A No, I'm going to be thin like my father.
Well, I'm going to go to lunch now.

2 *Going to* Future: Negative with *not*

Listen to these sentences. Then repeat them.

I'm going to ask some questions.

I'm not going to give the answers.

I'm going to study economics.

I'm not going to study engineering.

He's going to eat the dinner.

He's not going to cook it.

Her little girl is going to be fat.

She's not going to be thin.

We're going to have lunch there.

We're not going to have dinner there.

They're going to come back late tonight.

They're not going to come back early.

NEW VOCABULARY IN LESSON 21

NOUNS		VERBS	ADJECTIVES
art	flight	attend	fat
bell	news	drive	regional
cab	suit	report	thin
color	surprise		surprising
experiment			

GRAMMAR WORDS	EXPRESSIONS		NAMES

Prepositions:
  by
  like
	color TV
	do homework
	get late
	get married
		Guess what?
		work on
		report on
			Places:
			  Far East
			  Miami

LESSON 22

DIALOGS

Dialog 1: Driving to the Airport

Mrs. Watson is driving her husband to the airport. They are talking as they drive along.

MRS. WATSON   How are you going to get to Florida?

MR. WATSON   I'm taking a plane to Milwaukee.
From there I take a direct flight to Miami.

Watch out for that car!

(brakes screech)

MRS. WATSON   Oooh! That was close.

Well, there's the airport.
What time is it?

MR. WATSON   Just 7:40.

Dialog 2: At the Airport

Mr. and Mrs. Watson enter the airport. As they do, there is an announcement over the loudspeaker.

LOUDSPEAKER   *Attention, please. Central Airlines Flight 602 from Chicago. Now arriving at Gate 4.*

MRS. WATSON   *What airline are you taking?*

MR. WATSON   *Midwestern—Flight 543.*

MRS. WATSON   *You're going to call me tonight, aren't you?*

MR. WATSON   *Yes, of course.*
But it's going to be quite late.

LOUDSPEAKER   *This is the last call for Midwestern Airlines Flight 543 for Milwaukee.*
All passengers please board at Gate 2.

MRS. WATSON   *That's your plane, Bob.*
Take care of yourself.

MR. WATSON   *Okay. Good-bye. I'll call you.*

LOUDSPEAKER   *Passengers for Milwaukee Flight 543.*
Final boarding.

PRACTICE DRILLS AND EXERCISES

1 *Going to* Future: Tag Questions

Take the part of Speaker A. Form questions using negative tags.

AFFIRMATIVE STATEMENT
1. YOU'RE GOING TO CALL ME.
2. SHE'S GOING TO COME.
3. WE'RE GOING TO BE EARLY.
4. THEY'RE GOING TO TELL US.
5. MARY'S GOING TO HELP THEM.
6. TOM'S GOING TO ATTEND THE MEETING.

SPEAKER A NEGATIVE TAG	SPEAKER B EXPECTED SHORT ANSWER
1. *You're going to call me, aren't you?*	Yes, I am.
2. *She's going to come, isn't she?*	Yes, she is.
3. ....?	Yes, we are.
4. ....?	Yes, they are.
5. ....?	Yes, she is.
6. ....?	Yes, he is.

Take the part of Speaker A. Form questions using affirmative tags.

NEGATIVE STATEMENT
1. YOU AREN'T GOING TO BE LATE.
2. THEY'RE NOT GOING TO COME.
3. YOU AREN'T GOING TO TAKE A PLANE.
4. HE ISN'T GOING TO BE A DOCTOR.
5. ELLIE'S NOT GOING TO DO HER HOMEWORK.
6. WE'RE NOT GOING TO MISS THE PLANE.

| SPEAKER A | SPEAKER B |
| AFFIRMATIVE TAG | EXPECTED SHORT ANSWER |

1. *You aren't going to be late, are you?*   No, I'm not.
2. *They're not going to come, are they?*   No, they're not.
3. ....?   No, I'm not.
4. ....?   No, he isn't.
5. ....?   No, she isn't.
6. ....?   No, we're not.

2 Vocabulary: Practice with Opposites

Repeat these questions and answers.

Is it early?
    No, it's late.

Am I getting fat?
    No, you're getting thin.

Is that orange sweet?
    No, it's sour.

Is that lesson long?
    No, it's short.

Is your father a short man?
    No, he's tall.

Is that the question?
    No, that's the answer.

Is he old?
    No, he's young.

Is it a hard lesson?
    No, it's easy.

Is that hat new?
    No, it's old.

3 *Going to* Future: Affirmative Statement

Substitute the things that Mr. Watson is going to do.

MR. WATSON:

I'm going to *stay home tomorrow.*
I'm going to *be home all day.*
    (do a lot of things)
    (clean the garage)
    (fix the car)
    (take a long nap)

UNIT 6 LESSON 22 | 193

Substitute the things that Mrs. Watson is going to do.

MRS. WATSON:

I'm going to *do a lot of things tomorrow.*
I'm going to *take care of the children.*
............................*(clean the house)*
............................*(fix my hair)*
............................*(give a party at night)*

4 Conjunction (with Deletion): *and . . . too*

Listen to the models. Then make a third sentence.

1. He's going to stay at a hotel.
   I'm going to stay at a hotel, too.
   He's going to stay at a hotel and I am, too.

2. We're going to see him tomorrow.
   They're going to see him tomorrow, too.
   We're going to see him tomorrow, and they are, too.

3. Mary's going to call me.
   Helen's going to call me, too.

   ....

4. I'm going to go fishing.
   Tom's going to go fishing, too.

   ....

5. Ted's going to attend the meeting.
   We're going to attend the meeting, too.

   ....

5 Countries and Nationalities

Study this table.

COUNTRY	NATIONALITY	ONE PERSON
Korea	He's Korean.	He's a Korean.
Japan	He's Japanese.	He's a Japanese.
Thailand	She's Thai.	She's a Thai.
China	He's Chinese.	He's a Chinese.
Vietnam	He's Vietnamese.	He's a Vietnamese.
Italy	She's Italian.	She's an Italian.
Spain	He's Spanish.	He's a Spaniard.
Germany	He's German.	He's a German.
Norway	He's Norwegian.	He's a Norwegian.
Switzerland	He's Swiss.	He's a Swiss.
Canada	He's Canadian.	He's a Canadian.
the United States	He's American.	He's an American.
Mexico	He's Mexican.	He's a Mexican.
Costa Rica	He's Costa Rican.	He's a Costa Rican.
Colombia	She's Colombian.	She's a Colombian.

Substitute the countries and make the necessary changes in the second sentence.

My friend's from *Korea*.   He's a Korean.
My friend's from *Germany*. (Germany)   He's a German.
.... (Switzerland) ....
.... (the United States) ....
.... (Japan) ....
.... (Canada) ....
.... (Spain) ....
.... (Italy) ....
.... (Thailand) ....

UNIT 6 LESSON 22 | 195

6 Nationalities: Singular and Plural

Repeat the sentences. Read across.

ONE PERSON	MORE THAN ONE PERSON
He's a Korean.	They're Koreans.
She's a Japanese.	They're Japanese.
She's a Thai.	They're Thais.
He's a Chinese.	They're Chinese.
She's a Vietnamese.	They're Vietnamese.
She's an Italian.	They're Italians.
He's a Spaniard.	They're Spaniards.
He's a German.	They're Germans.
He's a Norwegian.	They're Norwegians.
I'm a Swiss.	We're Swiss.
I'm a Canadian.	We're Canadians.
She's an American.	They're Americans.
He's a Mexican.	They're Mexicans.
She's a Costa Rican.	They're Costa Ricans.
He's a Colombian.	They're Colombians.

Read the sentence. Then form a second sentence. Follow the models.

1. Jin and Sool are from Korea.   *They're Koreans.*
2. Miss Moon is from Korea.   *She's a Korean.*
3. Maria's from Spain.   ....
4. Carlos and Dolores are from Costa Rica.   ....
5. Mr. Wong's from China.   ....
6. Mr. Hanson's from Norway.   ....
7. Mr. Oda's from Japan.   ....
8. Mr. and Mrs. Ryerson are from Canada.   ....
9. Mr. Prado's from Colombia.   ....
10. Mr. and Mrs. Perez are from Spain.   ....

7 Countries and Nationalities

Read the first sentence. Then form a second sentence following the model. Use subject pronouns.

1. Mr. Prado's a Spaniard.   *He's from Spain.*
2. Mr. and Mrs. Garcia are Colombians. *They're from Colombia.*
3. Mrs. Switzer is a Swiss.   ....
4. Miss Suzuki's a Japanese.   ....
5. Mr. and Mrs. Hanson are Norwegians. ....
6. Miss Kim is a Korean.   ....
7. Miss Duc is a Vietnamese.   ....
8. Mr. and Mrs. Hunter are Canadians.   ....
9. Mr. and Mrs. Long are Americans.   ....
10. Mr. Rossi's an Italian.   ....
11. His wife's a Thai.   ....
12. Dolores is a Mexican.   ....
13. Mr. Guttag is a German.   ....
14. Miss Lu's a Chinese.   ....
15. Mr. and Mrs. Perez are Costa Ricans. ....

NEW VOCABULARY IN LESSON 22

NOUNS		VERBS	ADJECTIVES	
garage	plane	clean	close	sweet
hair	(airplane)	fix	Costa Rican	Swiss
nap	Spaniard	stay	direct	Vietnamese
orange	thing		sour	

COMPOUND	NAMES
airport	Masculine: Jin Sool
	Feminine: Duc
EXPRESSIONS	Family:
	Garcia Lu Ryerson
Oooh! take a flight	Guttag Moon Suzuki
take a nap take care of yourself	Hanson Prado Switzer
take a plane watch out for	Hunter Rossi Wong
	Place:
	Costa Rica Switzerland
	Florida Vietnam
	Milwaukee
	Company: Midwestern Airlines

LESSON 23

READING: A LETTER TO ALICE

Jim Carter and Alice Hayes became good friends while he was spending the summer with his sister and her husband in Madison, Wisconsin. He is now at the University of Chicago and corresponds regularly with Alice.

December 15

Dear Alice,

Thanks for your nice letter. It's always good to hear from you.

Today was the last day of my examinations. The exam in economics was quite difficult, but the others were easy. I'm ready for a vacation now, and I'm very anxious to see you and to be with you again.

I'm going to spend my Christmas and New Year's holidays in Madison with my sister Barbara and her husband. I'm going to fly to Madison this time. I'm not sure of the flight number, but I'm going to leave Chicago at 9:00 a.m.

Right now I'm going downtown. I'm going to shop for Christmas gifts. (I'm probably going to spend all my money.) I'm excited about Christmas, and about seeing you again.

Love,

Jim

PRACTICE DRILLS AND EXERCISES

1 *Going to* Future: Question-word (Wh-) Questions with *What*

Speaker A: Form a question using *What are you going to do?* + a time expression.
Speaker B: Respond with a short answer.

1. READ THE NEWSPAPER THIS MORNING

    SPEAKER A   *What are you going to do this morning?*
    SPEAKER B   *Read the newspaper.*

2. FIX THE CAR TODAY

    SPEAKER A   *What are you going to do today?*
    SPEAKER B   *Fix the car.*

3. CLEAN THE GARAGE ON SATURDAY

    SPEAKER A   ....?
    SPEAKER B   ....

4. STUDY FOR AN EXAM TONIGHT

    SPEAKER A   ....?
    SPEAKER B   ....

5. TAKE A VACATION NEXT MONTH

    SPEAKER A   ....?
    SPEAKER B   ....

6. TAKE MY SISTER TO THE AIRPORT RIGHT NOW

    SPEAKER A   ....?
    SPEAKER B   ....

7. TAKE A NAP THIS AFTERNOON

    SPEAKER A   ....?
    SPEAKER B   ....

8. GO TO A PARTY TONIGHT

    SPEAKER A ....?

    SPEAKER B ....

9. TAKE A TRIP TO JAPAN NEXT YEAR

    SPEAKER A ....?

    SPEAKER B ....

10. BUY A GIFT FOR MARY THIS AFTERNOON

    SPEAKER A ....?

    SPEAKER B ....

2 *Going to* Future: Question-word (Wh-) Questions with *Who*

Speaker A: Form a question using *who*. (Note: Use *who's* for every question.)
Speaker B: Give a short reply. Do not use pronoun subjects.

1. JOHN'S GOING TO TELL THEM THE BAD NEWS.

    SPEAKER A *Who's going to tell them the bad news?*

    SPEAKER B *John is.*

2. MARY AND ALICE ARE GOING TO GIVE THE PARTY FOR HELEN.

    SPEAKER A *Who's going to give the party for Helen?*

    SPEAKER B *Mary and Alice are.*

3. BARBARA AND THE CHILDREN ARE GOING TO MEET BOB AT THE AIRPORT.

    SPEAKER A ....?

    SPEAKER B ....

UNIT 6 LESSON 23 | 201

4. MRS. WATSON'S GOING TO CLEAN THE HOUSE.

   SPEAKER A ....?

   SPEAKER B ....

5. THE MECHANIC'S GOING TO FIX THE CAR.

   SPEAKER A ....?

   SPEAKER B ....

6. CHUCK AND BILL ARE GOING TO ATTEND THE MEETING.

   SPEAKER A ....?

   SPEAKER B ....

7. JANE'S GOING TO CALL US.

   SPEAKER A ....?

   SPEAKER B ....

8. ALICE IS GOING TO GET A SURPRISE.

   SPEAKER A ....?

   SPEAKER B ....

9. THE LINGS ARE GOING TO GO TO THE PARTY. .

   SPEAKER A ....?

   SPEAKER B ....

10. MISS LARSON'S GOING TO TYPE THE LETTERS.

    SPEAKER A ....?

    SPEAKER B ....

DIALOG FOR COMPREHENSION: MEETING ON THE STREET

Mrs. Watson and Alice Hayes are walking along the street when they see and greet each other.

Listen to this dialog several times. Make sure you understand it. Learn the new words.

MRS. WATSON	Hello, Alice.
ALICE	Why, hello, Mrs. Watson. How are you?
MRS. WATSON	Fine. Jim's coming Saturday for the holidays.
ALICE	Yes, I know. I have a letter from him right here. I'm so excited!
MRS. WATSON	I have a problem. I'm not going to be able to meet him.
ALICE	Oh, Dad's going to let me have the car on Saturday. I'll be glad to meet him.
MRS. WATSON	That's very helpful. Well, good-bye, Alice. It was very nice to see you.
ALICE	Good-bye, Mrs. Watson. See you Saturday.

GREETINGS, DEPARTURES, AND RESPONSES

1 Greetings and Responses

Study these greetings and replies. Then repeat them.

Good morning.
    Good morning.
    Hello.
    Good morning. How are you?
    Hello. How are you this morning?

Good afternoon.
    Good afternoon.
    Hello.
    Good afternoon. How are you today?
    Hello. How are you?

Good evening.
    Good evening.
    Hello.
    Good evening. How are you this evening?
    Hello, how are you?

Hello. (Hi.)
    Hello. (Hi.)
    Hello. How are you?
    (Hi there. How are you?)
    Hello. How are you this morning?
    Hello. How are you this afternoon?
    Hello. How are you this evening?

2 Greetings and Responses

Mr. Robert Watson is 35 years old. He works in a biological division of the government. During the day he sees various people. These are the people that he saw and the greetings that were used on one day.

7:30 a.m.

Mrs. Barbara Watson, wife

Good morning, Barb.
Good morning.

8:30 a.m.

Miss Elizabeth Larson, office typist

Good morning, Betty.
Good morning, Mr. Watson.

10:30 a.m.

Mr. Steven Park, co-worker and friend

Good morning, Steve.

Hello, Bob. How are you today?

2:00 p.m.

Mr. Lewis, Mr. Watson's superior in the office

Hello, Mr. Lewis.

Hello.

2:30 p.m.

Mr. Watson answering the telephone

Good afternoon.
This is Watson speaking.

4:00 p.m.

A friend in the office

Hello.
Hi, how are you?

UNIT 6 LESSON 23 | 205

6:00 p.m.

Mr. Watson's children

    Hi, Ellie.
    Hi, Tom.

    Hi, Daddy.

8:00 p.m.

Mrs. Smith, an acquaintance, walking along the street

Good evening, Mrs. Smith.

Good evening, Mr. Watson.
Nice evening, isn't it?

8:30 p.m.

A good friend in the neighborhood

    Hi.

    Hi. How are you?
    What's new?

3 Departures (1)

Study these departures and replies. Then repeat them.

Good-bye.
    Good-bye.
    Good-bye. I'll see you tomorrow.
    Good-bye. I'll see you soon.
    Good-bye. Call me next week.

Good night.
    Good night.
    Good-bye.
    Good night. I'll see you tomorrow.
    Good-bye. I'll see you soon.

INFORMAL
So long.
    So long.
    Good-bye.
    So long. See you later.
    Good-bye. I'll see you tomorrow.

4 Departures (2)

Mrs. Barbara Watson sees and then says good-bye to several people during the day. These are brief exchanges that took place one day.

8:00 a.m.

Her husband goes to work.

Good-bye, dear.
Good-bye.
See you tonight.

8:30 a.m.

Tom, her 4-year-old boy, goes to school.

So long, Mom.
Good-bye, honey.
Have a good day.

9:30 a.m.

She talks to a good friend on the telephone.

Well, good-bye, Barb.

Good-bye, Helen.
Thanks for calling.

3:00 p.m.

She meets Alice on the street.

Well, good-bye, Alice.
It was nice to see you.

Good-bye, Mrs. Watson.
See you Saturday.

5:00 p.m.

Mrs. Irene Ling leaves after a visit.

So long, Barb.

Good-bye, Irene.
See you tomorrow.

7:00 p.m.

Her daughter goes to a friend's house.

Good-bye, Mom.
I'm going to Kathy's house.

Good-bye, Ellie.
Be home by eight.

8:00 p.m.

*Her 4-year-old son
goes to bed.*

Good night, Tommy.
Sleep tight.

Good night, Mom.

9:00 p.m.

*Mrs. Jane Carlson
leaves after a visit.*

Good night, Barbara.

Good-bye, Jane.
It was nice to see you.

11:00 p.m.

Mrs. Watson goes to bed.

Good night, Bob.
I'm going to bed.

Good night, Barb.

NEW VOCABULARY IN LESSON 23

NOUNS		VERBS	ADJECTIVES	ADVERB
Christmas	mechanic	fly	anxious	probably
exam	problem	spend	helpful	
examination	trip			
holiday	vacation			

GRAMMAR WORD	COMPOUNDS	EXPRESSIONS	
Noun Substitute: others	airplane Christmas gift flight number New Year's	be able to be (so) excited be sure of get a surprise Good night. go to bed Hi, there.	honey New Year's holiday Sleep tight. take a trip take a vacation What's new? So long.

LESSON 24

LISTENING PRACTICE: AT THE AIRPORT

Mrs. Watson and the two children, Ellie and Tom, are at the airport in Madison, Wisconsin. They went to meet Mr. Watson. He has been at a conference in Miami, Florida.

LOUDSPEAKER	*Your attention, please. Central Airlines Flight 401 for Chicago. Now boarding at Gate 3.*
TOM	When's Daddy coming, Mom?
MRS. WATSON	In a few minutes, dear.
ELLIE	He's on Flight 641. That arrives at 5:30. It's going to come in at Gate 5.
TOM	When are we going to go on an airplane, Mom?
LOUDSPEAKER	*Midwestern Airlines Flight 641 from Milwaukee... Now arriving at Gate 5.*
MRS. WATSON	Where's Gate 5?
ELLIE	There it is, over there.
MRS. WATSON	Come on, children.
TOM	When are we going to go on an airplane, Mom?
MRS. WATSON	Soon, I hope, Tommy. Ask your Daddy.
LOUDSPEAKER	*Calling Dr. Nelson...Dr. James Nelson. Please call your office.*

ELLIE	There's Dad!
MRS. WATSON	Here, Bob! Over here!
MR. WATSON	Well, isn't this a nice surprise! Hi, Tommy.
TOM	Daddy?
MR. WATSON	Yes, Tommy?
TOM	When are we going to go on an airplane?
MR. WATSON	Well, I don't know, son. Soon, I hope. Hello, dear. Say, where's the car?

PRACTICE DRILLS AND EXERCISES

1 First Names: Diminutive Forms

Study these forms.

MASCULINE			FEMININE		
FULL NAME	SHORT FORM	DIMINUTIVE	FULL NAME	SHORT FORM	DIMINUTIVE
Thomas	Tom	Tommy	Margaret	Marge	Margie
Robert	Bob	Bobby	Katherine	Kate	Kathy
William	Bill	Billy	Susan	Sue	Susie
James	Jim	Jimmy	Dorothy	Dot	Dotty
Kenneth	Ken	Kenny	Patricia	Pat	Patty/Patsy
Frederick	Fred	Freddy	Barbara	Barb	Barbie
John	Jack	Johnny/Jackie	Constance	-	Connie
Alan	Al	-	Rebecca	-	Becky
Philip	Phil	-	Adele	-	-
Gary	-	-	Mary	-	-
Glenn	-	-	Olga	-	-
Duane	-	-			

Listen to these exchanges.

THOMAS (AGE 4)	Hi, Billy.
WILLIAM (AGE 5)	Hi, Tommy.
ROBERT (AGE 35)	Hi, Bill.
WILLIAM (AGE 34)	Hello, Bobby.
PATRICIA (AGE 50)	Good morning, Connie.
CONSTANCE (AGE 45)	Good morning, Patsy.
ROBERT WATSON (AGE 33)	Hi, Al.
ALAN LONG (AGE 8)	Hello, Mr. Watson.
KENNETH (AGE 60)	Good night, Marge.
MARGARET (AGE 58)	Good night, Ken.
REBECCA (AGE 23)	Hi, Freddy.
FREDERICK (AGE 25)	Hi, Becky.

2 *Going to* Future: Question-word (Wh-) Questions with *When*

Speaker A: Form a question using *when*.
Speaker B: Reply with a short answer.

1. WE'RE GOING TO TAKE AN AIRPLANE TRIP NEXT MONTH.

   A *When are we going to take an airplane trip?*
   B *Next month.*

2. I'M GOING TO LEAVE FOR THE MEETING IN A FEW MINUTES.

   A *When are you going to leave for the meeting?*
   B *In a few minutes.*

3. MR. WATSON'S GOING TO CALL HIS WIFE FROM MIAMI AT ABOUT ONE A.M.

   A .... ?
   B ....

4. WE'RE GOING TO LEAVE AT FIVE IN THE MORNING.

   A .... ?
   B ....

UNIT 6 LESSON 24 | 213

5. JANE'S GOING TO CALL TOMORROW MORNING.

   A ....?
   B ....

6. THE CHILDREN ARE GOING TO GO TO THE PARTY AT TWO THIS AFTERNOON.

   A ....?
   B ....

7. JIM'S GOING TO LEAVE CHICAGO AT NINE A.M. ON SATURDAY.

   A ....?
   B ....

8. ALICE IS GOING TO MEET JIM AT THE AIRPORT ON SATURDAY MORNING.

   A ....?
   B ....

9. WE'RE GOING TO HAVE LUNCH AT TWELVE O'CLOCK SHARP.

   A ....?
   B ....

10. THE PLANE'S GOING TO ARRIVE IN TEN MINUTES.

    A ....?
    B ....

3 *Going to* Future: Question-word (Wh-) Questions with *Where*

Take the part of Speaker A. Form a question using *where*.

1. WE'RE GOING TO SPEND OUR VACATION IN COSTA RICA.

   A *Where are we going to spend our vacation?*
   B *In Costa Rica.*

2. I'M GOING TO EAT DOWNTOWN.

   A *Where are you going to eat?*
   B *Downtown.*

214 | UNIT 6 LESSON 24

3. HE'S GOING TO TAKE HIS CAR TO A GOOD MECHANIC.

   A ....?

   B ....

4. SHE'S GOING TO MEET HER HUSBAND AT THE AIRPORT.

   A ....?

   B ....

5. WE'RE GOING TO HAVE LUNCH IN A NICE RESTAURANT.

   A ....?

   B ....

6. MR. WATSON'S GOING TO ATTEND A MEETING IN MIAMI.

   A ....?

   B ....

7. THE MOVIE'S GOING TO BE AT THE NATIONAL THEATER.

   A ....?

   B ....

8. WE'RE GOING TO MEET HER AT THE ORIENTAL RESTAURANT.

   A ....?

   B ....

9. THEY'RE GOING TO STAY IN A GOOD HOTEL.

   A ....?

   B ....

10. BARBARA'S GOING TO HAVE THE PARTY AT HER HOUSE.

    A ....?

    B ....

4 *Going to* Future: Question-word (Wh-) Questions with *Who/What/When/Where*

Speaker A: Form a question with the question word that is given.
Speaker B: Reply with a short answer.

1. MARY'S GOING TO TYPE THE LETTER TO TOM.
   A *What is Mary going to type?*
   B *The letter to Tom.*

2. JOHN'S GOING TO COME TOMORROW.
   A *Who's going to come tomorrow?*
   B *John is.*

3. MR. AND MRS. WATSON ARE GOING TO VISIT US SOON.
   A *When* .... ?
   B ....

4. WE'RE GOING TO MEET THEM AT MING'S RESTAURANT.
   A *Where* .... ?
   B ....

5. MR. WATSON'S GOING TO READ THE REPORT.
   A *What* .... ?
   B ....

6. MRS. WATSON'S GOING TO DRIVE TO THE AIRPORT.
   A *Who* .... ?
   B ....

7. JIM'S GOING TO LEAVE CHICAGO AT NINE A.M.
   A *When* .... ?
   B ....

8. ALICE IS GOING TO MEET JIM AT THE AIRPORT.

   A *Where* .... ?

   B ....

9. MARY'S GOING TO CALL US AT NOON.

   A *When* .... ?

   B ....

10. MR. LONG'S GOING TO TAKE A PLANE TO TORONTO.

    A *Who* .... ?

    B ....

11. WE'RE GOING TO MEET THEM AT THE HOTEL.

    A *Where* .... ?

    B ....

12. JOHN'S GOING TO BUY A NEW HAT TOMORROW.

    A *What* .... ?

    B ....

13. JIM'S GOING TO BUY ALICE A SURPRISE.

    A *Who* .... ?

    B ....

5 *There's going to be...*

Substitute the noun phrases.

There's going to be a *party*.
There's going to be a *birthday party*. *(birthday party)*
.... *(party for Helen)*
.... *(dinner party)*
.... *(surprise party)*

UNIT 6 LESSON 24 | 217

6 Is there going to be . . . ?

Speaker A: Form a yes/no question. Leave out the time or place expression.
Speaker B: Give a short answer. Follow the models.

1. THERE'S GOING TO BE A PARTY TONIGHT.

    A *Is there going to be a party?*
    B *Yes. Tonight.*

2. THERE'S GOING TO BE A MEETING IN NEW YORK.

    A *Is there going to be a meeting?*
    B *Yes. In New York.*

3. THERE'S GOING TO BE A SURPRISE PARTY AT 8 O'CLOCK.

    A . . . . ?
    B . . . .

4. THERE'S GOING TO BE AN OFFICE MEETING AT 2 O'CLOCK.

    A . . . . ?
    B . . . .

5. THERE'S GOING TO BE A DINNER PARTY ON SATURDAY.

    A . . . . ?
    B . . . .

6. THERE'S GOING TO BE A STAFF MEETING IN MY OFFICE.

    A . . . . ?
    B . . . .

7. THERE'S GOING TO BE A BIRTHDAY PARTY TUESDAY.

    A . . . . ?
    B . . . .

8. THERE'S GOING TO BE A RESEARCH MEETING NEXT WEEK.

   A .... ?

   B ....

9. THERE'S GOING TO BE A BUSINESS MEETING IN ROOM 424.

   A .... ?

   B ....

10. THERE'S GOING TO BE A REGIONAL MEETING IN MIAMI.

    A .... ?

    B ....

7 Conjoining with *and*

Construct a sentence using *First . . . and then . . . .* Follow the models.

1. READ THE NEWSPAPER/TAKE A NAP
   First I'm going to read the newspaper, and then I'm going to take a nap.

2. FIX THE CAR/TAKE A RIDE
   First I'm going to fix the car, and then I'm going to take a ride.

3. CALL A CAB/GO TO THE AIRPORT

   ....

4. EAT DINNER/WATCH TV

   ....

5. GO HOME/GO OUT TO DINNER

   ....

UNIT 6 LESSON 24 | 219

6. WRITE A LETTER/READ

   . . . .

7. ATTEND THE STAFF MEETING/GO TO LUNCH

   . . . .

8. SEE FRIENDS IN ARGENTINA/VISIT MY FAMILY IN BRAZIL

   . . . .

NEW VOCABULARY IN LESSON 24

NOUNS	ADJECTIVE	ADVERBS	EXPRESSIONS
gate restaurant theater	national	first then	over here take a ride

COMPOUNDS	NAMES

airplane trip
business meeting
office meeting
research meeting
surprise party
	Diminutive Masculine:
	  Billy Freddy Jimmy
	  Bobby Jackie Kenny
	Diminutive Feminine:
	  Becky Dottie Patsy Susie
	  Connie Margie Patty
	Company Names:
	  Ming's Restaurant
	  National Theater
	  Oriental Restaurant

APPENDIX

A. Names of Days
   Sunday   Monday   Tuesday   Wednesday   Thursday   Friday   Saturday

B. Names of Months
January	April	July	October
February	May	August	November
March	June	September	December

C. Cardinal Numbers

one	eleven	twenty-one	thirty-one
two	twelve	twenty-two	thirty-two
three	thirteen	twenty-three	(etc.)
four	fourteen	twenty-four	forty
five	fifteen	twenty-five	fifty
six	sixteen	twenty-six	sixty
seven	seventeen	twenty-seven	seventy
eight	eighteen	twenty-eight	eighty
nine	nineteen	twenty-nine	ninety
ten	twenty	thirty	one hundred

D. Ordinal Numbers

first	eleventh	twenty-first	thirty-first
second	twelfth	twenty-second	thirty-second
third	thirteenth	twenty-third	(etc.)
fourth	fourteenth	twenty-fourth	fortieth
fifth	fifteenth	twenty-fifth	fiftieth
sixth	sixteenth	twenty-sixth	sixtieth
seventh	seventeenth	twenty-seventh	seventieth
eighth	eighteenth	twenty-eighth	eightieth
ninth	nineteenth	twenty-ninth	ninetieth
tenth	twentieth	thirtieth	one hundredth

E. Family Names (Names in E, F, G likely to be names of people whose background is other than English, Irish or Scottish are indicated in the parentheses.)

Bellini (It.)	Hill	Martin	Ross
Black	Hudson	Mason	Rossi (It.)
Brown	Hunter	Moon (Kor.)	Ryerson
Caine	Jennings	Morley	Smith
Carlson (Swed.)	Johnson	Morton	Stewart
Carter	Jones	Murray	Strong
Chang (Chi.)	Kao (Chi.)	Nelson	Suzuki (Jap.)
Clark	Kelly	Oda (Jap.)	Swenson (Swed.)
Durand (Fr.)	Kimura (Jap.)	Okayama (Jap.)	Switzer (Swiss)
Evers	King	Olson (Scan.)	Taylor
Foster	Larson (Scan.)	Park	Todd
Fuller	Lee	Parker	Watson
Garcia (Sp.)	Lewis	Penney	Weiss (Ger.)
Green	Ling (Chi.)	Perez (Sp.)	Wheeler
Guttag (Ger.)	Long	Platte	Wilson
Hamm (Ger.)	Loo (Chi.)	Porter	Wong (Chi.)
Hanson (Nor.)	Lopez (Sp.)	Prado (Sp.)	Wood
Hayes	Low	Ramos (Sp.)	Yamato (Jap.)
High	Lu (Chi.)	Rodriguez (Sp.)	Yang (Chi.)

F. Masculine Given Names (Only the names in italic were used actively.)

Alan, *Al*	Gary	Philip, *Phil*
Carlos (Sp.)	Glenn	*Robert, Bob, Bobby*
Charles, *Chuck*	*Hugo* (Lat.)	*Rodney, Rod*
Dick	James, *Jim, Jimmy*	Roy
Don	*Jin* (Kor.)	*Sool* (Kor.)
Duane	*John, Jack,* Johnny, *Jackie*	Steven, *Steve*
Edward, *Ed*	Kenneth, Ken, Kenny	*Ted*
Edwin, *Ed*	Larry	Thomas, *Tom, Tommy*
Eric (Scan.)	*Luis*	Walt
Frederick, *Fred, Freddy*	Owen	William, Bill, Billy

APPENDIX | 223

G. Feminine Given Names (Only the names in italic were used actively.)

Adele	Elizabeth, *Betty*	Margaret, *Marge*, Margie
Alice	*Ella*	*Maria* (Sp.)
Anita	*Helen*	*Mary*
Ann	*Irene*	*Mercedes* (Sp.)
Barbara, Barb, Barbie	*Jane*	*Nancy*
Catherine, Cathy	*Jo*	Olga
Constance, *Connie*	Katherine, Kate, Kathy	*Pamela*
Dolores	*Kathleen, Kathy*	Patricia, Pat, Patty, *Patsy*
Dorothy, Dot, Dotty, Dottie	Kim (Kor.)	Rebecca, *Becky*
Duc (Viet.)	*Laura*	Susan, Sue, Susie
Eleanor, *Ellie*	*Lydia*	

H. Names of Cities (Cities in the United States and Canada are indicated.)

Amsterdam	London	Osaka	Rome
Bangkok	Los Angeles (U.S.)	Oslo	Santiago
Berlin	Madison (U.S.)	Ottawa (Can.)	Seoul
Bogotá	Madrid	Paris	Singapore
Brasilia	Miami (U.S.)	Peking	Stockholm
Caracas	Mexico City	Phnom Penh	Tokyo
Chicago (U.S.)	Milwaukee (U.S.)	Rangoon	Toronto (Can.)
Denver (U.S.)	Montreal (Can.)	Recife	Valparaiso
Lisbon	New York (U.S.)	Rio de Janeiro	Washington, D.C. (U.S.)

I. Names of Countries, Adjectives of Nationality (Words in parentheses are not used in this book.)

COUNTRY	NATIONALITY	COUNTRY	NATIONALITY
Argentina	(Argentine)	Italy	Italian
Australia	Australian	Japan	Japanese
Brazil	Brazilian	Korea	Korean
Burma	Burmese	Mexico	Mexican
Cambodia	Cambodian	Netherlands	Dutch
Canada	Canadian	Norway	Norwegian
Chile	(Chilean)	Spain	Spanish
China	Chinese	Sweden	Swedish
Colombia	Colombian	Switzerland	Swiss
Costa Rica	Costa Rican	Thailand	Thai
England	English	United States	American
France	French	Venezuela	Venezuelan
Germany	German	Vietnam	Vietnamese
Honduras	(Honduran)	(Ireland)	Irish

J. Other Names

> States of the U.S.: Colorado, Florida, Minnesota, New York, Wisconsin
>
> Regions of the World: Africa, Central America, Far East, South America
>
> Companies: Lamar Lumber Company, Midwestern Airlines, National Theater, Orient Airlines, Oriental Restaurant, Ming's Restaurant
>
> School: University of Chicago
>
> Words Used as Names of Streets: Branch, Clayton, Fall, First, Flower, Jefferson, Main, Oak, River, Rose, Western

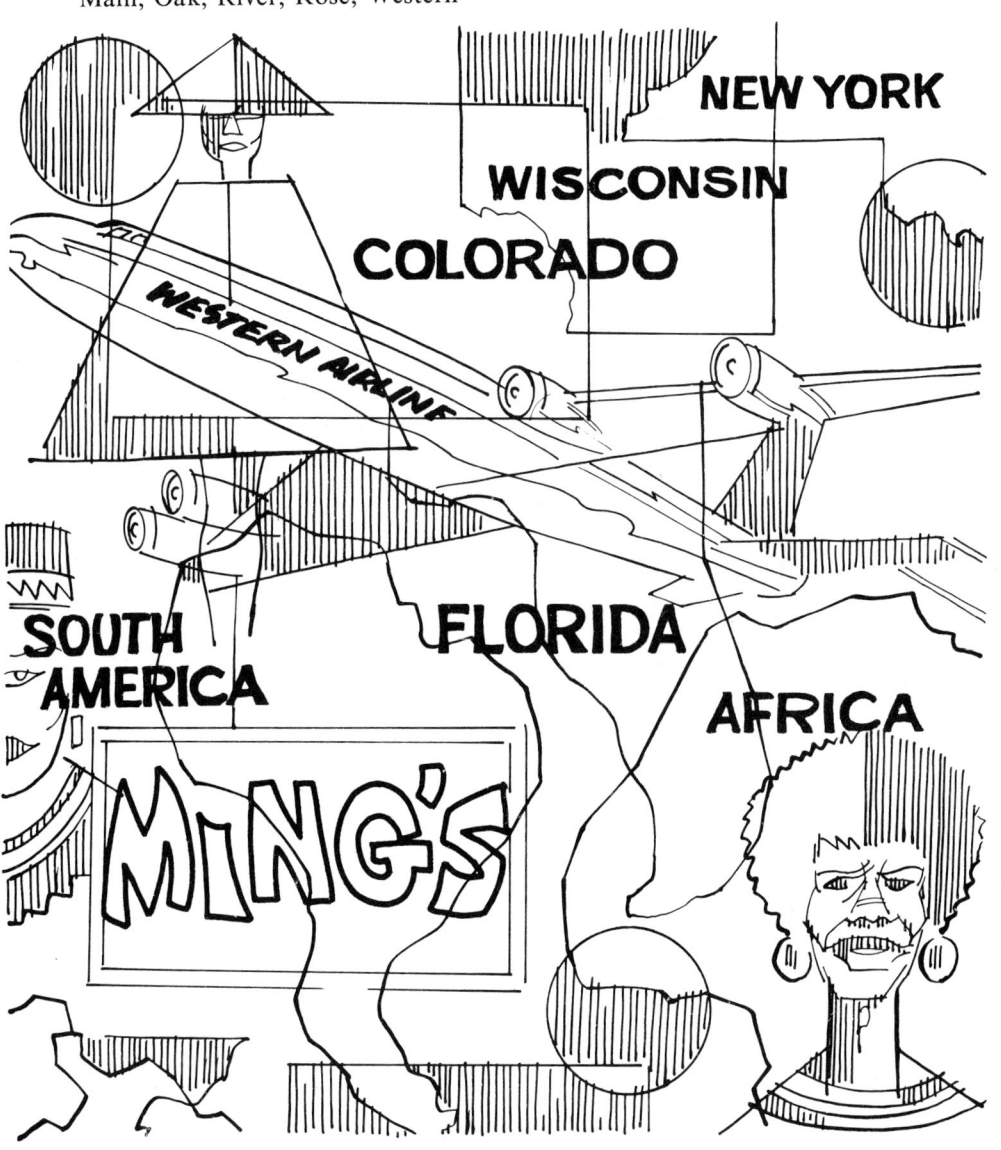

INDEX

This index shows where to find practice material on the grammatical points and situation topics covered in *Welcome to English Book 1*. The references are to the practices that deal most specifically with the topic in question. A few additional examples can usually be found in Dialogs and Readings near the page references cited.

Addresses [80]

Age [76, 163]

Alphabet [83]

An and *A* [17]

Birthday [80, 88]

Cardinal Numbers [67, 70, 75-76]
    (For uses see Addresses, Age, Dates, Designation, Enumeration, Telling Time.)

Compounds [24]

Conjunctions:
    And [43, 111]; *And . . . too* (with deletion) [81, 131, 194]
    But [89, 109]; *But* (with deletion) [135]
    First . . . and then [219]; Semicolon (;) [116]

Continuous Tense: (See Past Continuous, Present Continuous)

Contractions:
    Contractions of *BE* and *Not* are used throughout the book. These are only the references in the first unit in which they occur.
    BE forms Attached to Pronoun [7-8, 10, 15-17]
    Is Attached to Name [14]
    Is Attached to Question Words [9-10, 12, 23-24, 26, 117, 118, 119]
    Is Attached to *There* [165-166, 170-171]
    Isn't/Aren't [41, 43, 54]
    Wasn't/Weren't [73-74, 82, 88-89]
    I'd [34]; *I'll/We'll* [118]

Counting [67, 70, 75-76]

Dates [79, 86-89]

Days [114-116]

Demonstratives:
    Pronouns *This, That* [4, 8-10, 15, 18-19, 22-24]
        These, Those [26, 46-48]
    Determiners [9-10, 35, 37, 48]

Departures [206, 211]

Designation by Cardinal Number [68]

Determiners:
    An and *A* [17]
    Demonstratives [9-10, 35, 37, 48]
    Possessives [141]
    Some and *Any* [144-146, 157, 170, 172]
    What + Country [128]; *What + Day* [114]
    This, Last, Next, Every (in time expressions) [86, 88-89, 109, 115]

Did and *Didn't* [77-78]

Diminutive Names [211-212]

Do and *Does* [81]

Echo Questions [184]

Enumeration (Telling how many) [68, 77]

Future:
    BE + -Ing form [117-119]
    Will + Verb (only *I'll, We'll*) [118]
    Going to + Verb [181, 186, 192, 193-194, 199-200, 212-218]

Greetings [3, 12, 203-205, 212-213]

Identifying People [9-10, 46, 48]

Identifying Things [23, 26, 46-47]

Imperative Expressions [8]

-Ing Verb Form [97]

Interested Comment (in form of negative yes/no question) [59]

Intonation:
    Statements [3, 14, 25, 109, 184, 186]
    Yes/No Questions [3, 18-19, 27, 54, 102, 106, 166, 183]
    Tag Questions [141, 166, 175]
    Short Answers [18, 27-28, 200-202]
    Question-word Questions [3, 23-24, 97, 181, 200-202]
    Conjunction [131, 135]
    Interested Comment (as negative yes/no question) [59]
    Echo Question [184]
    Noun Compounds [24]
    Contrastive Intonation [25, 60, 88, 102, 122, 130-131, 135]
    In Counting [67, 70]
    In Greetings [3, 12]
    In Introductions [33]
    In Street Addresses [80]

Introductions [33]

Let's + Verb [134]

Months [86]

Mass Nouns:
    Some as determiner for indefinite amount [144-146, 157]
    Some and *Any* determiners [170, 172]
    Counters (for definite amount) [144, 146-147, 154, 157]

Names (See Day, Months, Nationality, Personal Names)

Nationality:
    Adjective [53-54, 85, 127]
    Noun [195-197]

Negative:
    Statements [41, 43, 184, 188]
    Short Answers [36, 40-41, 74, 115]
    Yes/No Questions [53-54, 82]
    In Conjunctions [43, 89, 109, 116]
    In Interested Comment [59]

Nouns (See Determiners, Mass Nouns, Plural of Nouns, Compounds)

Numbers (See Cardinal Numbers, Ordinal Numbers)

Occupations [49-51, 130, 149-150]

One as Substitute Word [164]

Opposites (of vocabulary words) [193]

Ordinal Numbers [86-87]

Past Continuous [110-111, 118]

Personal Names:
    Full Names [35-37]
    Short and Diminutive Forms [58-59, 212-213]

Plural of Nouns:
    S-Form [15]; Irregular [55]; Nationalities [196]

Polite Expressions for Visiting [90]

Possessive Determiners [160]

Present Continuous [98, 106, 117-118]

Present Tense:
    Plain Form Only—Contrasted with Present Continuous [109]

Pronoun Substitution:
    Subject Pronouns Only
    [8, 10, 12, 40, 51, 60, 76, 82, 116, 127-128, 130, 150, 163, 184, 196-197]
    (Also, many "Short Answer" exercises involve substitution.)

Pronunciation:
    Contracted *Is* [14]; -Ing Verb Form [97]
    Noun Plural [15]; 13 and 30 etc. [77]

Question-word Questions:
    What [23, 50-51, 130, 150, 200]; *What country* [128]
    Who [9, 48, 201]
    When [80, 115, 117, 213]
    Where [214]
    How [12]; *How old* [163]; *How many* [171, 173]; *How much* [173]
    What/Who [24, 46, 60]; *What/Where* [26]; *What/When/Where* [81, 128]

Short Answers:
    Intonation [18, 27]
    To Yes/No Question [18-19, 27-28, 40, 74, 111]
    To Negative Yes/No Question [54]
    To Question-word Question [118-120, 200-201, 213, 216]

Spelling [83]

Statements: Intonation and Basic Form [4, 14, 22, 66]

Tag Questions:
    Negative Tag [141, 160]; Affirmative Tag [151]
    Negative and Affirmative Tags [174-175, 192]; *There is* [166]

Telling Time [95-97, 99, 101]

There as Place Substitute [115]

There in Subject Position [86]

Verb Form: -Ing Form [97]

Verb-Subject Agreement [41, 54, 81, 88-89]

Will + Verb (*I'll, We'll* only) [118]

Yes/No Questions
    Intonation of [3, 18-19, 27]
    Formation of [40-41, 74, 81, 106, 111, 193, 218]
    Negative [53-54, 82, 115]

GRAMMAR POINTS

UNIT 1
Lessons 1, 2, 3, 4

Verb *BE*
AFFIRMATIVE STATEMENTS

Contractions			Full Forms		
SUBJECT + BE	COMPLEMENT		SUBJECT	BE	COMPLEMENT
I'm			I	am	
He's She's It's	here.		He She It	is	here.
We're You're They're			We You They	are	

SHORT ANSWERS

YES	SUBJECT	BE
Yes,	I	am.
	he/she/it	is.
	we/you/they	are.

QUESTION-WORD QUESTIONS

QUESTION WORD	BE	SUBJECT
Who	am	I?
What	is	he/she/it?
Where	are	we/you/they?
etc.		

YES/NO QUESTIONS

BE	SUBJECT	COMPLEMENT
Am	I	
Is	he/she/it	here?
Are	we/you/they	

UNIT 2
Lessons 5, 6, 7, 8

Verb *BE*
NEGATIVE STATEMENTS

Full Form			
SUBJECT	BE	NOT	COMPLEMENT
I	am	not	here.
He/She/It	is		
We/You/They	are		

Contractions: Form 1		
SUBJECT + BE	NOT	COMPLEMENT
I'm	not	here.
He's/She's/It's		
We're/You're/They're		

Contractions: Form 2		
SUBJECT*	BE + N'T	COMPLEMENT
He/She/It	isn't	here.
We/You/They	aren't	

*Forms with subject *I* do not occur in this frame.

GRAMMAR POINTS | 231

Verb *BE*
NEGATIVE QUESTIONS

BE + N'T	SUBJECT*	COMPLEMENT
Isn't	he/she/it	right?
Aren't	we/you/they/I	

*The subject *I* (with *aren't*) occurs infrequently in present tense negative questions for most speakers. A tag question *(I'm right, aren't I?)* is often used in its place. *Am I not right?* is considered more formal usage.

Verb *BE*
NEGATIVE SHORT ANSWERS
FORM 1

NO	SUBJECT + BE	NOT
No,	I'm	not.
	he's/she's/it's	
	we're/you're/they're	

FORM 2

NO	SUBJECT*	BE + N'T
No,	he/she/it	isn't.
	we/you/they	aren't.

*Forms with subject *I* do not occur in this frame.

232 | GRAMMAR POINTS

UNIT 3
Lessons 9, 10, 11, 12

Verb *BE:* Past Tense

AFFIRMATIVE STATEMENT

SUBJECT	BE	COMPLEMENT
I/He/She/It	was	here.
We/You/They	were	

NEGATIVE STATEMENT

SUBJECT	BE + NOT	COMPLEMENT
I/He/She/It	wasn't	here.
We/You/They	weren't	

AFFIRMATIVE YES/NO QUESTION

BE	SUBJECT	COMPLEMENT
Was	I/he/she/it	here?
Were	we/you/they	

NEGATIVE YES/NO QUESTION

BE + N'T	SUBJECT	COMPLEMENT
Wasn't	I/he/she/it	here?
Weren't	we/you/they	

AFFIRMATIVE SHORT ANSWER

YES	SUBJECT	BE
Yes,	I/he/she/it	was.
	we/you/they	were.

NEGATIVE SHORT ANSWER

NO	SUBJECT	BE + N'T
No,	I/he/she/it	wasn't.
	we/you/they	weren't.

GRAMMAR POINTS | 233

UNIT 4
Lessons 13, 14, 15, 16

Continuous

	Present		
	SUBJECT + BE	-ING FORM	COMPLEMENT
AFFIRMATIVE STATEMENT	He's	studying	English.
NEGATIVE STATEMENT	He isn't		
AFFIRMATIVE YES/NO QUESTION	Is he	studying	English?
NEGATIVE YES/NO QUESTION	Isn't he		

	Past		
	FORM OF BE	-ING FORM	COMPLEMENT
AFFIRMATIVE STATEMENT	He was	studying	English.
NEGATIVE STATEMENT	He wasn't		
AFFIRMATIVE YES/NO QUESTION	Was he	studying	English?
NEGATIVE YES/NO QUESTION	Wasn't he		

Present Continuous and Present Tense: Contrast

Present Tense *Every Day*	**Present Continuous** *Now*
I study. We practice. They work.	I'm studying. We're practicing. They're working.

UNIT 5
Lessons 17, 18, 19, 20

Verb *BE*

	Tag Question for Affirmative Statement					Expected Answer			
	SUBJECT	BE	COMPL.	TAG QUESTION	YES	SUBJECT	BE
PRESENT	I	am	here,	aren't I?	Yes,	you	are.
	He/She/It	is		isn't he/she/it?		he/she/it	is.
	We/You/They	are		aren't we/you/they?		you/we/they	are.
PAST	I/He/She/It	was	here,	wasn't I/he/she/it?	Yes,	you/he/she/it	were/was.
	We/You/They	were		weren't we/you/they?		you/we/they	were.

	Tag Question for Negative Statement					Expected Answer			
	SUBJECT	BE + NOT / N'T	COMPL.	TAG QUESTION	NO	SUBJECT	BE + N'T
PRESENT	I	'm not	here,	am I?	No,	you	aren't.
	He/She/It	isn't		is he/she/it?		he/she/it	isn't.
	We/You/They	aren't		are we/you/they?		you/we/they	aren't.
PAST	I/He/She/It	wasn't	here,	was I/he/she/it?	No,	you/he/she/it	weren't/wasn't.
	We/You/They	weren't		were we/you/they?		you/we/they	weren't.

GRAMMAR POINTS | 235

UNIT 6
Lessons 21, 22, 23, 24

GOING TO Future

	SUBJECT + BE	GOING TO	VERB	COMPLEMENT
AFFIRMATIVE	He's	going to	study	English.
NEGATIVE	He's not/He isn't			
AFFIRMATIVE YES/NO QUESTION	Is he	going to	study	English?
NEGATIVE YES/NO QUESTION	Isn't he			

GOING TO Future with Tag Question

	SUBJECT + BE	GOING TO + VERB + COMPL.	TAG QUESTION
AFFIRMATIVE	I'm	going to be here,	aren't I?
	He's/She's/It's		isn't he/she/it?
	We're/You're/They're		aren't we/you/they?
NEGATIVE	I'm not	going to be here,	am I?
	He's/She's/It's not		is he/she/it?
	We're/You're/They're not		are we/you/they?

236 | GRAMMAR POINTS

VOCABULARY

This is a list of all the vocabulary items of *Welcome to English Book 1*. It does not include names, place names and nationalities. These are listed in the Appendix. The lesson in which each item first occurs is indicated by number.

a [1]
   a few minutes [13]
   a great idea [16]
   a lot of [16]
about [13]
absent [10]
accountant [7]
actually [19]
address *(n)* [11]
after [13]
   afternoon [9]
again [2]
airline [7]
airplane [22]
   airplane trip [24]
airport [22]
all day [9]
   all day today [10]
   all kinds [18]
   all over [18]
   all right [8]
almost [13]
also [6]
always [14]
am [1]
a.m. [13]
an [3]
   an hour late [9]
and [1]
angry [20]
anxious [23]
any [13]
   anybody [13]
are [1]
   aren't [6]
architect [18]

architecture [18]
army officer [18]
art [21]
artist [3]
at *(place)* [7]
at *(time)* [9]
   at least [19]
   at night [13]
attend [21]
avenue [11]

back *(adv)* [15]
bar *(of soap)* [18]
be able to *(+ verb)* [23]
   be any good [20]
   be born [11]
   be *(so)* excited [23]
   be fun [16]
   be married [3]
   be served [20]
   be sure of [23]
   be tired [13]
   be upset [19]
beautiful [14]
because [18]
bed [4]
believe [9]
bell [21]
best [3]
better [9]
   better than [20]
bicycle [13]
big [4]
biologist [7]
biology [20]

birthday [7]
   birthday card [7]
   birthday party [15]
bit *(small amount)* [17]
black [17]
blue [4]
book [2]
both [11]
bottle [17]
bowl [18]
box [18]
boy [2]
bread [18]
   breadbox [20]
breakfast [17]
brother [3]
building [11]
business [4]
   business letter [4]
   business meeting [24]
   businessman [8]
busy [9]
but [10]
butter [18]
buy [13]
by [21]
   by the way [15]
'Bye. [14]

cab *(taxi)* [21]
cake *(of soap)* [18]
calendar [15]
call [5]
   Call me Barbara. [5]
Can you spell . . . ? [11]

captain [18]
car [17]
card [7]
cassette [4]
   cassette tape
     recorder [4]
cereal [18]
certainly [7]
chair [6]
chalk [18]
chemist [5]
chemistry [20]
child, children [8]
Christmas [23]
   Christmas gift [23]
city [10]
civil engineer [18]
class [4]
clean (v) [22]
clerk [18]
clock [4]
close (v) [2]
close (adj) [22]
clothes [13]
coat [12]
coffee [17]
cold (adj) [17]
color [21]
   color TV [21]
come [2]
   Come in. [2]
   Come on. [13]
company [7]
continue [9]
conversation [9]
cook (n, v) [14]
cookie [14]
country (nation) [19]
country (rural) [14]
crazy [15]
cream [17]
cube (of butter) [18]

cup [17]
cupboard [20]

Dad [20]
Daddy [20]
dance (v) [14]
date [12]
daughter [3]
day [10]
Dear (+ Name), [19]
dentist [2]
department [18]
desk [3]
dialog [9]
difficult [16]
dinner [4]
   dinner guest [4]
   dinner party [12]
direct (adj) [22]
dirty [18]
do [5]
   do homework [21]
   do research [16]
doctor [2]
does [7]
door [19]
down (adv) [2]
   downtown [11]
Dr. [5]
drink [17]
drive [21]

early [9]
easy [10]
eat [14]
economics [20]
economist [11]
education [18]
efficient [17]
electronics [18]
employee [11]
engineer [3]

engineering [18]
English (language) [3]
   English book [4]
   English professor [4]
   English teacher [3]
enjoy [11]
eraser [19]
especially [14]
evening [13]
every [10]
every day [10]
exactly [12]
exam [23]
examination [23]
Excuse me. [3]
experiment [21]

family [2]
famous [16]
farm (n, v) [14]
   farmhouse [14]
farmer [18]
fat [21]
father [12]
feel [9]
field (occupation) [18]
file clerk [19]
fine [1]
fireman [8]
first (adv) [24]
fish (n) [15]
   fish (v) [13]
fix [22]
flight [21]
   flight number [23]
fly [23]
foot [19]
for [6]
   for the summer [6]
fortunate [18]
French (language) [15]
   French toast [18]

fresh [17]
friend [1]
from [5]
fruit [17]
   fruit juice [17]
full name [5]
fun [16]

game [14]
garage [22]
gate [24]
genetics [16]
get [15]
   get a surprise [23]
   get acquainted [6]
   get late [21]
   get married [21]
gift [7]
give a paper [16]
   give a report [17]
girl [2]
glad [5]
glass *(container)* [17]
go [15]
   go fishing [16]
   go to bed [23]
good [1]
   Good-bye. [14]
   Good luck. [17]
   Good morning. [1]
   Good night. [23]
government [7]
grandfather [14]
grandmother [14]
grandparent [14]
green [4]
groceries [13]
guess *(v)* [13]
   Guess what? [21]
guest [4]

Ha. [3]
hair [22]
half [13]
   half past *(one)* [13]
hand [18]
hard *(difficult)* [19]
hat [19]
have [6]
   have a good time [19]
   have a party [15]
   have dinner [15]
   have fun [16]
   have no idea [19]
   have trouble with [14]
he [1]
   he's [1]
hear [19]
Hello. [1]
help [1]
helpful [23]
her [3]
here [3]
heredity [16]
Hi. [8]
   Hi, there. [23]
his [4]
history [14]
   history lesson [14]
holiday [23]
home [6]
   homework [19]
honey *(dear)* [23]
hope [9]
hospital [6]
hot [17]
hotel [10]
hour [9]
house [11]
   household [18]
how [1]
   How are you? [1]
   How do you do? [5]

How do you
   spell . . . ? [11]
how many [19]
how much [20]
how old [9]
how's [2]
hundreds [19]
hungry [13]
husband [6]

I [1]
   I can't believe it. [17]
   I don't know. [10]
   I guess not. [13]
   I'll [15]
   I'll miss you. [16]
   I'm [1]
   I'm *(so)* glad you
      could come. [12]
idea [13]
imagine [8]
   Imagine that! [8]
important [16]
introduce [8]
in *(adv)* [1]
in *(prep)* [3]
   in an hour [15]
   in bed [4]
   in class [4]
instant coffee [20]
interesting [5]
is [1]
   isn't [5]
it [2]
   It doesn't matter. [17]
   it's [2]
   It's good to see you. [2]

jar [18]
jelly [18]
juice [17]
just [1]

VOCABULARY | 239

just fine [1]

kind *(n)* [18]
kitchen [19]
know [5]

lady [8]
lake [13]
lane [11]
large [6]
last *(adj)* [5]
   last week [9]
late [9]
later [14]
law [3]
   law book [4]
   law professor [3]
lawyer [1]
leave [13]
lesson [9]
let [12]
   Let me take your
     coat. [12]
Let's see. [13]
letter [4]
lift off *(n)* [9]
like *(v)* [5]
like *(prep)* [21]
listen [2]
little [7]
live [6]
living room [13]
loaf, loaves [18]
look [8]
   look for [14]
lots of fun [16]
love [19]
luck [13]
lumber [7]
   lumber company [7]
lump [17]
lunch [15]

make [12]
   Make yourself at
     home. [12]
man [2]
map [4]
math [15]
May I have . . . ? [17]
   May I help you? [1]
maybe [9]
me [13]
meal [17]
mechanic [23]
medical [16]
   medical doctor [16]
   medical student [20]
medicine [18]
meet [5]
meeting [15]
men [8]
middle [5]
midnight [15]
milk [17]
minute [8]
miss [16]
Miss *(title)* [1]
missing *(adj)* [19]
Mmm! [18]
Mom [14]
Mommy [16]
month [12]
morning [1]
mother [4]
movie [13]
Mr. [1]
Mrs. [1]
Ms. [2]
my [2]
My! [8]

name [1]
nap [22]
national [24]

nationality [10]
near [12]
need *(v)* [17]
neighbor [7]
new [2]
   New Year's [23]
news [21]
   newspaper [13]
next [12]
nice [2]
niece [15]
night [10]
no [3]
noon [13]
not [3]
now [3]
number [9]
nurse [2]
nursery school [3]

occupation [7]
o'clock [9]
   (one) o'clock
     sharp [13]
of [3]
   of course [13]
office [1]
   office building [11]
   office meeting [24]
   office visitor [1]
officer [18]
Oh! [3]
Okay. [8]
old [2]
on [3]
   on time [9]
ones *(n. sub.)* [13]
only [9]
Oooh! [22]
open [2]
or [17]
orange [22]

other [18]
others [23]
our [6]
out [6]
    out of town [20]
over *(adv)* [2]
    over here [24]
    over there [2]

package [13]
page [9]
paper [18]
parent [16]
party [12]
past *(prep)* [13]
pen [4]
pencil [4]
people [3]
perhaps [19]
person [3]
phone *(n)* [14]
physicist [16]
picture [3]
piece [18]
plan *(v)* [15]
plane *(airplane)* [22]
play *(v)* [14]
    play tennis [16]
please [1]
p.m. [13]
policeman [8]
portable radio [4]
pot [17]
pound [18]
practice *(n)* [9]
    practice *(v)* [13]
    practice law [3]
president [7]
pretty *(adj)* [8]
    pretty *(intensifier)* [13]
probably [23]
problem [23]
profession [18]

professor [2]
program [19]

quarter [13]
question [9]
quite [9]

radio [4]
read [13]
ready [14]
red [4]
regional [21]
remember [8]
repeat [2]
    Repeat after me. [2]
report *(n)* [14]
    report *(v)* [21]
    report on [21]
research *(n)* [16]
    research meeting [24]
restaurant [24]
rice [20]
ride *(v)* [13]
right *(correct)* [8]
    right there [16]
road [11]
room [4]
ruler [19]
run *(of a watch)* [17]

sandwich [15]
say [9]
Say! [2]
school [3]
science [3]
    science book [4]
    science professor [4]
    science teacher [3]
scientist [1]
secretary [1]
see [2]
    see *(understand)* [15]

sentence [2]
set the table [20]
she [1]
    she's [2]
sheet *(of paper)* [18]
shirt [19]
shoe [19]
shop *(v)* [13]
short [8]
show *(v)* [5]
sick [9]
sing [14]
sister [3]
sit [2]
    sit down [2]
Sleep tight. [23]
slice [18]
slow [17]
small [4]
So long. [23]
soap [18]
sock [19]
some [17]
sometimes [17]
son [3]
soon [19]
sorry [5]
soup [20]
sour [22]
Spaniard [22]
speak [10]
spell [11]
spend [23]
staff meeting [17]
start *(v)* [2]
state *(of the U.S.)* [6]
stay [22]
stick *(of butter)* [18]
still *(adv)* [14]
stocking [19]
stop *(v)* [2]

VOCABULARY | 241

store *(n)* [18]
street [11]
student [1]
study [9]
subject [19]
sugar [17]
suit [21]
summer [6]
suppose [15]
sure [15]
surprise *(n)* [21]
   surprise party [24]
surprising [21]
sweet [22]

table [4]
take [12]
   take *(+ course)* [20]
   take a nap [22]
   take a plane [22]
   take a ride [24]
   take a trip [23]
   take a vacation [23]
   take care of [14]
   take care of
     yourself [22]
   take flight *(+ number)* [22]
talk [3]
tall [8]
tape [2]
   tape recorder [2]
tea [17]
teacher [1]
teaching *(n)* [18]
telephone [4]
   telephone
     conversation [14]
tennis [16]
textbook [7]
Thank you. [1]
Thanks. [1]

that [2]
   that's [2]
the [4]
   the day after
     tomorrow [15]
   the other day [18]
theater [24]
their [13]
them [14]
then [24]
there *(place)* [1]
   there are [12]
these [4]
they [3]
   they'll [13]
   they're [3]
thin [21]
thing [22]
think [17]
this [1]
   this morning [1]
those [4]
three [9]
time [13]
to [6]
   to *(infinitive*
     particle) [2]
toast [18]
today [9]
together [19]
tomorrow [12]
tonight [13]
too [3]
town [12]
train [15]
trip [23]
trouble [14]
Tuesday of next week [15]
TV [13]
type *(v)* [13]
   typewriter [4]
typist [1]

uncle [7]
understand [10]
university [7]
upstairs [6]
us [13]
use *(v)* [17]
usually [9]

vacation [23]
very [1]
   very much [6]
   very well [1]
vice-president [18]
visit *(v)* [14]
visitor [1]

walk [13]
wall [4]
want [5]
was [9]
   wasn't [10]
wash [18]
watch *(n)* [9]
   watch *(v)* [13]
   watch out for [22]
water [17]
we [3]
   we'll [15]
   we're [3]
week [9]
   weekend [15]
Well, [5]
well *(adv)* [1]
were [9]
   weren't [10]
western [11]
what [4]
   what's [4]
   What's new? [23]
   What's the matter? [18]
when [11]
where [3]

where's [4]
white [18]
  white bread [18]
who [2]
  who's [2]
Why! [17]
wife [3]
. . . will you? [14]
window [19]
with [6]
woman [2], women [8]
word [2]
work *(v)* [6]
  work on [21]
worker [20]
Wow! [18]
write [19]
wrong [15]

year [10]
yellow [18]
yes [1]
  Yes, please. [1]
yesterday [9]
yet [13]
you [1]
  you're [3]
  You're all wrong. [15]
  You're not kidding me. [20]
  You're welcome. [16]
young [3]
your [2]

zero [12]